Experimenting with Everyday Science

Food

Stephen M. Tomecek

CHELSEA HOUSE
PUBLISHERS
An imprint of Infobase Publishing

To my good friend Barbara Santino,
who has helped me "cook up" a lot of great experiments
over the years. Thanks for being there when I needed you!

Experimenting with Everyday Science: Food

Copyright © 2010 by Infobase Publishing

Chelsea House
An imprint of Infobase Publishing
132 West 31st Street
New York NY 10001

Library of Congress Cataloging-in-Publication Data
Tomecek, Steve.
 Food / Stephen M. Tomecek.
   p. cm. — (Experimenting with everyday science)
 Includes bibliographical references and index.
 ISBN 978-1-60413-173-4 (hardcover)
 1. Food—Analysis—Juvenile literature. 2. Food—Composition—Juvenile literature. I. Title. II. Series.
 TX533.T66 2010
 641.3—dc22   2010005691

Chelsea House books are available at special discounts when purchased in bulk quantities for businesses, associations, institutions, or sales promotions. Please call our Special Sales Department in New York at (212) 967-8800 or (800) 322-8755.

You can find Chelsea House on the World Wide Web at http://www.chelseahouse.com.

Text design by Annie O'Donnell
Cover design by Alicia Post
Composition by Mary Susan Ryan-Flynn
Illustrations by Sholto Ainslie for Infobase Publishing
Cover printed by Bang Printing, Brainerd, MN
Book printed and bound by Bang Printing, Brainerd, MN
Date printed: September 2010
Printed in the United States of America

10 9 8 7 6 5 4 3 2 1

Contents

Introduction

When you hear the word *science*, what's the first thing that comes to mind? If you are like most people, it's probably an image of a laboratory filled with tons of glassware and lots of sophisticated equipment. The person doing the science is almost always wearing a white lab coat and probably is looking rather serious while engaged in some type of experiment. While there are many places where this traditional view of a scientist still holds true, labs aren't the only place where science is at work. Science can also be found at construction sites, on a basketball court, and at a concert by your favorite band. The truth of the matter is that science is happening all around us. It's at work in the kitchen when we cook a meal, and we can even use it when we paint a picture. Architects use science when they design a building, and science also explains why your favorite baseball player can hit a homerun.

In **Experimenting with Everyday Science**, we are going to examine some of the science that we use in our day-to-day lives. Instead of just talking about the science, these books are designed to put the science right in your hands. Each book contains about 25 experiments centering on one specific theme. Most of the materials used in the experiments are things that you can commonly find around your house or school. Once you are finished experimenting, it is our hope that you will have a better understanding of how the world around you works. While reading these books may not make you a world-class athlete or the next top chef, we hope that they inspire you to discover more about the science behind everyday things and encourage you to make the world a better place!

Safety Precautions

REVIEW BEFORE STARTING ANY EXPERIMENT

Each experiment includes special safety precautions that are relevant to that particular project. These do not include all the basic safety precautions that are necessary whenever you are working on a scientific experiment. For this reason, it is necessary that you read and remain mindful of the General Safety Precautions that follow.

Experimental science can be dangerous, and good laboratory procedure always includes carefully following basic safety rules. Things can happen very quickly while you are performing an experiment. Materials can spill, break, or even catch fire. There will be no time after the fact to protect yourself. Always prepare for unexpected dangers by following the basic safety guidelines during the entire experiment, whether or not something seems dangerous to you at a given moment.

We have been quite sparing in prescribing safety precautions for the individual experiments. For one reason, we want you to take very seriously every safety precaution that is printed in this book. If you see it written here, you can be sure that it is here because it is absolutely critical.

Read the safety precautions here and at the beginning of each experiment before performing each activity. It is difficult to remember a long set of general rules. By rereading these general precautions every time you set up an experiment, you will be reminding yourself that lab safety is critically important. In addition, use your good judgment and pay close attention when performing potentially dangerous procedures. Just because the text does not say "be careful with hot liquids" or "don't cut yourself with a knife" does not mean that you can be careless when boiling water or punching holes in plastic bottles. Notes in the text are special precautions to which you must pay special attention.

GENERAL SAFETY PRECAUTIONS

Accidents caused by carelessness, haste, insufficient knowledge, or taking an unnecessary risk can be avoided by practicing safety procedures and being alert while conducting experiments. Be sure to check the individual experiments in this book for additional safety regulations and adult supervision requirements. If you will be working in a lab, do not work alone. When you are working off site, keep in groups with a minimum of three students per group, and follow school rules and state legal requirements for the number of supervisors required. Ask an adult supervisor with basic training in first aid to carry a small first-aid kit. Make sure everyone knows where this person will be during the experiment.

PREPARING

- Clear all surfaces before beginning experiments.
- Read the instructions before you start.
- Know the hazards of the experiments and anticipate dangers.

PROTECTING YOURSELF

- Follow the directions step-by-step.
- Do only one experiment at a time.
- Locate exits, fire blanket and extinguisher, master gas and electricity shut-offs, eyewash, and first-aid kit.
- Make sure there is adequate ventilation.
- Do not horseplay.
- Keep floor and workspace neat, clean, and dry.
- Clean up spills immediately.
- If glassware breaks, do not clean it up; ask for teacher assistance.
- Tie back long hair.
- Never eat, drink, or smoke in the laboratory or workspace.
- Do not eat or drink any substances tested unless expressly permitted to do so by a knowledgeable adult.

USING EQUIPMENT WITH CARE

- Set up apparatus far from the edge of the desk.
- Use knives or other sharp-pointed instruments with care.
- Pull plugs, not cords, when removing electrical plugs.
- Clean glassware before and after use.
- Check glassware for scratches, cracks, and sharp edges.
- Clean up broken glassware immediately.
- Do not use reflected sunlight to illuminate your microscope.
- Do not touch metal conductors.
- Use alcohol-filled thermometers, not mercury-filled thermometers.

USING CHEMICALS

- Never taste or inhale chemicals.
- Label all bottles and apparatus containing chemicals.
- Read labels carefully.
- Avoid chemical contact with skin and eyes (wear safety glasses, lab apron, and gloves).
- Do not touch chemical solutions.
- Wash hands before and after using solutions.
- Wipe up spills thoroughly.

HEATING SUBSTANCES

- Wear safety glasses, apron, and gloves when boiling water.
- Keep your face away from test tubes and beakers.
- Use test tubes, beakers, and other glassware made of Pyrex glass.
- Never leave apparatus unattended.
- Use safety tongs and heat-resistant gloves.

- If your laboratory does not have heat-proof workbenches, put your Bunsen burner on a heat-proof mat before lighting it.
- Take care when lighting your Bunsen burner; light it with the airhole closed, and use a Bunsen burner lighter in preference to wooden matches.
- Turn off hot plates, Bunsen burners, and gas when you are done.
- Keep flammable substances away from flames and other sources of heat.
- Have a fire extinguisher on hand.

FINISHING UP

- Thoroughly clean your work area and any glassware used.
- Wash your hands.
- Be careful not to return chemicals or contaminated reagents to the wrong containers.
- Do not dispose of materials in the sink unless instructed to do so.
- Clean up all residues and put them in proper containers for disposal.
- Dispose of all chemicals according to all local, state, and federal laws.

BE SAFETY CONSCIOUS AT ALL TIMES!

The Need for Food

Do you like to eat? Most people do. Whether it's a five-course dinner at a fancy restaurant, a bowl of cereal for breakfast, or just a slice of pizza, eating is a big part of our lives. We don't generally think about it, but a lot has to happen before we can take a bite out of an apple or nosh on a chicken nugget. Before food can be eaten, it must be produced, processed, and prepared. All of these steps involve some type of science. When farmers grow crops, they use their knowledge of biology and ecology. When a chef whips up a new recipe, he or she uses the rules of chemistry and an understanding of how matter changes. Even frying an egg requires a basic understanding of physics and heat transfer.

There are many places where science and food are connected. Any type of food can help satisfy hunger, but foods have different effects on the body. The science of **nutrition** is all about understanding what food is made of and how our bodies use it. Sometimes even food that starts out being healthy can be harmful to us if it is not prepared or preserved properly. **Microbiology** is the study of tiny living things, including bacteria and fungi, that can invade our food and cause it to spoil.

What follows is an examination of how science comes into play in the production, preparation, and preservation of food. Rather than just explaining these connections, you will have the opportunity to discover them for yourself by doing experiments as you read. As you might have guessed, many of these experiments will require you to work with food. In some cases, you will even get to taste your experiment as you go. Whether you are experimenting in your kitchen at home or in a lab at school, it is important that you always follow the safety instructions. Also, be sure that all surfaces and utensils are clean, both before and after each experiment. This will help your science experiments to be both safe and satisfying!

Carbon dioxide and water produce carbohydrates in the chlorophyll-containing tissues of plants that are exposed to sunlight. Chlorophyll is the green substance found mainly in the chloroplasts of plants.

ENERGY FROM FOOD

Eating is much more than one of the "simple pleasures" of life. As members of the animal kingdom, humans need to eat. All of the **energy** that we require to keep our bodies functioning well comes from food. This makes us different from most plants. Green plants have the ability to tap into energy from the Sun and to make their own food by a process called **photosynthesis.** Plants get energy from sunlight, water, carbon dioxide in the air, and **nutrients** from the soil. Nutrients are chemical substances that living things need to survive. We will begin our investigation of food with a look at how vegetables and fruit are produced. In **Experiment 1:** *How Soil Nutrients Affect Plant Growth*, you will test the effect that different levels of soil nutrients have on plant growth.

EXPERIMENT 1

How Soil Nutrients Affect Plant Growth

Topic

How does the level of soil nutrients affect plant growth?

Introduction

Unlike animals or fungi, green plants have the ability to manufacture their own food from sunlight, carbon dioxide, and water using a process called photosynthesis. In order for plants to have sustained healthy growth, they also require a number of substances called nutrients. Nutrients usually come from the soil. In this activity, you are going to test to see how different levels of soil nutrients affect the growth of plants in a controlled experiment.

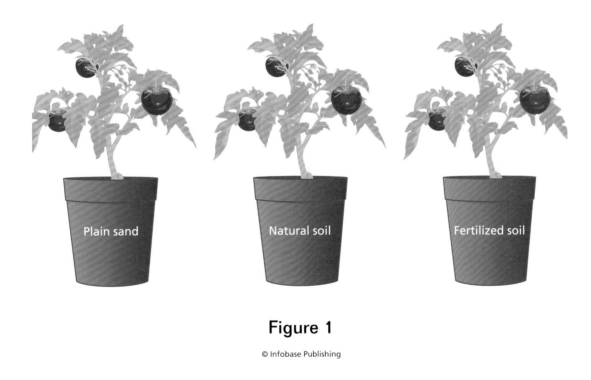

Plain sand

Natural soil

Fertilized soil

Figure 1

Time Required

30 minutes for set-up, 3 weeks for observation

Materials

- 3 small plastic or ceramic flower pots, all the same size

- 2 cups (500 mL) fine, washed sand

- 4 cups (1 L) natural soil or potting soil mix

- 3 tomato seedlings, all about 6 in. (15 cm) tall

- small box of Miracle Gro or similar plant food with an N-P-K rating of 5-10-5 (available at most nurseries or garden stores)

- masking tape

- marking pen

- ruler

- measuring cup

- water

- sunny windowsill or counter big enough to hold all three flower pots

Safety Note No special safety precautions are needed for this activity. Please review and follow the safety guidelines before proceeding.

Procedure

1. Use the masking tape to label the first pot "plain sand," the second pot "natural soil," and the third pot "fertilized soil." Fill the "natural soil" pot about ¾ full with soil. Fill the "plain sand" pot with the same amount of sand. Fill the pot labeled "fertilized soil" with the same amount of soil. Follow the directions on the fertilizer package and add fertilizer to the pot labeled "fertilized soil." Place one tomato seedling in each of the three pots. Make certain that the plant roots are buried to the same depth in each pot. Add ½ cup (125 mL) water to each pot and place them next to each other on a sunny windowsill.

2. Use the ruler to measure the height of each plant and record the information on the data table.

3. Every three days, add ½ cup (125 mL) of water to each pot and record the plant heights on the data sheet, along with any other observations concerning their growth. After 21 days, make your final observations about the growth and health of each plant.

Data Table 1			
	Height of Plants		
	Plain sand	**Natural soil**	**Fertilized soil**
Day 1			
Day 4			
Day 7			
Day 10			
Day 13			
Day 16			
Day 19			
Day 21			

Analysis

1. Why is it important that each plant receive the same amounts of water and sunlight during the experiment?
2. Which plant showed the most growth after 21 days? Which plant showed the least amount of growth?
3. What role did the fertilizer provide?

 ## What's Going On?

Even though green plants have the ability to manufacture their own food by photosynthesis, most plants also require certain nutrients in order to maintain healthy growth. These nutrients are usually provided by the soil and are taken in by plant roots. Soil nutrients are chemical compounds that come either from minerals released when rock breaks down, or from decaying organic material, such as dead animals and leaves. Three of the most important soil nutrients are nitrogen, phosphorus, and potassium. Nitrogen is important for good leaf growth. Without it, plants will be stunted and leaves will turn yellow. Phosphorus is important for root growth and plant vigor. Potassium, which is also called potash, helps to stimulate seed growth and makes a plant mature faster.

In a natural garden, soil, nitrogen, phosphorus, and potassium are usually present in sufficient quantities to maintain healthy plant growth. Plain sand, however, has almost none of these nutrients. As a result, most plants grown in sand alone show very poor growth and often die after a few weeks even if they get enough water and sunlight. Adding fertilizer to nutrient-poor soil will allow plants to grow better. The fertilizer provides the nutrients that are normally missing.

Commercial plant food is designed to provide the macronutrients of nitrogen, phosphorus and potassium, plus several other micronutrients, which are also important for healthy growth. The labels on commercial fertilizers tell you which nutrients they contain and their percentages. Since nitrogen, phosphorus, and potassium are the nutrients required in the highest amounts, the percentage of each is listed in large numbers on the top of the fertilizer label. A fertilizer marked as 5-10-5 contains 5% nitrogen, 10% phosphorus, and 5% potassium.

Our Findings

1. In a controlled experiment, all of the variables must be the same except for the one that you are testing. In this experiment, all conditions have to be the same except for the soil in which the plants are growing.

2. Answers will vary depending on the type of soil used, but the plant in the fertilized soil should have shown the best growth. The plant in the plain sand should have showed minimal growth and may have died.

3. The fertilizer provided extra nutrients that are normally present in natural soil.

CHAIN OF FOODS

When it comes to food energy, all animals, including humans, are classified as **consumers.** Consumers cannot make their own food. Instead, they rely on living things called **producers** to meet their energy needs. Producers use photosynthesis to convert the Sun's energy into chemical compounds, which are then eaten by consumers. In some cases, an animal might eat a producer directly. A deer eats grass and leaves, which contain stored chemical energy. In other cases, a consumer may get its energy by eating another consumer. When a coyote eats a deer, it is acting as a "secondary consumer." The original energy that the grass took from the Sun is passed on to the coyote through the deer. The multiple relationships among living things eating one another are called a **food chain.**

Humans are part of thousands of food chains. In fact, almost everything we eat can be traced back to the Sun through a series of consumers and producers. Take a slice of pizza, for instance. A basic pizza is made from tomato sauce, cheese, and bread dough. Bread is made from wheat, which is a plant. The tomatoes used to make the sauce also come from plants. For both of these foods, you are the first level or "primary" consumer in the chain. Cheese, on the other hand, comes from milk, which most often comes from a cow. In this food chain, you are the secondary consumer. If you happen to like anchovies on your pizza (some people really do), then you are eating a fish, which ate tiny sea creatures, which ate photosynthetic algae. In this case, you are the "tertiary," or third-level, consumer. That means that every time you eat a slice of anchovy pizza, you are part of four different food chains.

In the real world, simple food chains are hard to come by. Most organisms are connected to a great many other living things. Cows aren't eaten only by humans, and they eat more than just grass. A cow can be connected to many different plants and animals. As a result, scientists usually speak about **food webs.** Food webs are far more complicated than simple food chains, but in the end, the energy they pass along can usually be traced back to the Sun.

CALORIES FROM FOOD

Each type of food you eat has a different amount of energy stored in it. Though a hot dog and a carrot weigh about the same, the hot dog contains about eight times more chemical energy than the carrot. When scientists talk about the energy in food, they use a unit called a **calorie.** In **Experiment 2:** *Measuring Energy Stored in Foods,* you will measure the number of calories found in different foods by turning the stored chemical energy into heat.

Measuring Energy Stored in Foods

Topic

How can you measure the amount of energy stored in different foods?

Introduction

All of the food that we eat contains stored chemical energy. Scientists measure this energy using a unit of heat called a calorie. One calorie is defined as the amount of heat energy needed to raise the temperature of 1 gram (g) of water by 1 degree Celsius. Calories are always calculated using the metric system. In this experiment, you will measure the number of calories found in three samples of food by converting their stored chemical energy into heat.

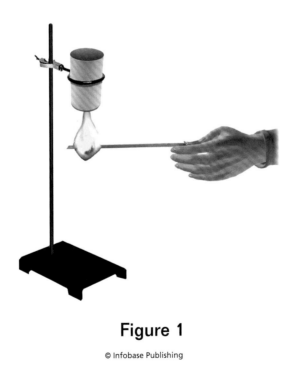

Figure 1

© Infobase Publishing

Time Required

60 minutes

Materials

- gram scale

- metal barbeque skewer

- ring stand

- small, empty steel soup can with label removed

- candle or Bunsen burner

- Celsius lab thermometer

- clock with second hand

- graduated cylinder or metric measuring cup

- ceramic dish

- large marshmallow

- piece of dried bread cut into a 1-in. (2.5-cm) cube

- piece of dried, hard cheese (Swiss or cheddar) cut into a 1-in. (2.5-cm) cube

- matches or lighter

- calculator

Safety Note During this experiment, you will be using an open flame to burn pieces of food. The tests should be conducted under the guidance of a responsible adult in an area that has a fireproof surface and is well ventilated. Please review and follow the safety guidelines before proceeding.

Procedure

1. Secure the empty soup can to the clamp in the ring stand and set the height so that the bottom of the can is about 6 in. (15 cm) above the table. If conducting the experiment at home, you can hold up the can with a heavy wire screen or small oven rack supported by two bricks. Use the graduated cylinder or measuring cup to pour 3.4 fl oz (100 mL) of water into the soup can.

2. Place the thermometer in the water and allow it to rest for one minute. Remove the thermometer and record the water temperature on the data table for "Dry Bread" next to the heading "Starting water temperature." Put the thermometer back into the can with the water.

3. Place the dried bread cube on the gram scale and weigh it. Record the weight on the data table under heading "mass of sample."

4. Have an adult place the bread cube on the end of the barbeque skewer. Have the adult light the Bunsen burner or candle and place it on the counter at least 2 ft (60 cm) away from the metal can. This will prevent heat from the flame from affecting the water temperature in the can. Use the skewer to hold the bread in the flame. As soon as the bread starts burning, move it directly under the metal can so that the flame it produces heats the water in the can. Do not move the bread until it is completely burned. If the flame should go out before the bread is burned, quickly relight it and continue to heat the water in the can. Once the flame has gone out, place the burned bread on the dish.

5. Remove the thermometer from the can and record the water temperature on the data table under the heading "Ending water temperature." Empty the water from the can and replace it with 3.4 fl oz (100 mL) of cool tap water.

6. Repeat Steps 2 to 5 using the dried cheese and the marshmallow. Record all your observations on the data table. After you have tested the marshmallow, calculate the number of calories found in each food sample by multiplying the change in water temperature by 100, which is the mass of the water in the can. After you have calculated the total number of calories per sample, divide the total calories by the mass of the sample to get the number of calories per gram of food.

Data Table 1
DRY BREAD
Mass of sample _____ grams
Ending water temperature _____ degrees C
Starting water temperature _____ degrees C
Change in water temperature _____ degrees C
Total number of calories in sample (change in water temperature x 100) _____ calories
Number of calories per gram weight of sample (total number of calories in sample/mass of sample) _____ calories/gram

DRY HARD CHEESE
Mass of sample _____ grams
Ending water temperature _____ degrees C
Starting water temperature _____ degrees C
Change in water temperature _____ degrees C
Total number of calories in sample (change in water temperature x 100) _____ calories
Number of calories per gram weight of sample (total number of calories in sample/mass of sample) _____ calories/gram
MARSHMALLOW
Mass of sample _____ grams
Ending water temperature _____ degrees C
Starting water temperature _____ degrees C
Change in water temperature _____ degrees C
Total number of calories in sample (change in water temperature x 100)_____ calories
Number of calories per gram weight of sample (total number of calories in sample/mass of sample) _____ calories/gram

Analysis

1. Which sample of food burned the slowest?
2. Which sample of food contained the most calories per gram?
3. Why is it important to divide the total number of calories found in the sample by the mass of the sample?
4. What is the mass of the water in the soup can?

 ## What's Going On?

Each type of food that we eat contains a different amount of stored energy. In order to accurately measure the total amount of stored energy found in different foods, technicians working in labs use a device called a bomb calorimeter. Food is placed in a chamber, and oxygen is pumped into the chamber. An electric current is used to ignite the food. As the food burns, it heats water that is contained in a jacket surrounding the chamber. In order to capture all of the heat from the food, the entire device is insulated so that no heat is lost to the outside air. Multiplying the change in water temperature by the mass of the water in the jacket gives the total number of calories.

When scientists measure the amount of chemical energy stored in foods, they usually use a unit called a **kilocalorie,** which is equal to 1,000 calories. Instead of writing the word kilocalorie, a more common approach is to simply write the word *Calorie* (with a capital C). When the caloric values of different foods are listed in charts or on food packages, they are given based on the mass of the food. This way, you can easily compare foods. For example, the total number of calories in a large apple might be the same as one small cookie, but the cookie will have more calories per gram.

Knowing the number of calories in the food you eat is important for maintaining a healthy body. As you go about your daily activities, the cells of your body burn the calories found in food, just like the engine of a car burns gasoline to make it go. If you do not take in enough calories from food, the cells of your body will run out of fuel. Yet if you take in more calories than your body needs, the excess will get stored as fat.

Our Findings

1. The piece of cheese should have taken the longest to burn, and the marshmallow should have burned the fastest.
2. The cheese should have contained the most calories per gram, followed by the bread and the marshmallow.
3. Dividing the total number of calories found in the food sample by the mass of the sample allows you to make an accurate comparison of the caloric value of each type of food.
4. The mass of the water in the soup can is 100 g (3.5 oz). In the metric system, 1 mL (0.03 fl oz) of water has a mass of 1 g (0.04 oz).

GOOD NUTRITION: YOU ARE WHAT YOU EAT

In the previous experiment, we saw how foods contain different amounts of calories. Eating the proper amount of calories each day is important for maintaining good health. However, the number of calories you eat is only half the story. The sources of the calories are just as important. Food is more than just an energy source for your body. It also affects the way you feel, the way you look, and the way you act. Food supplies your body with the raw materials it needs to grow and to repair damaged or dead cells. In short, food supplies your body with almost all of the proper nutrients. In the same way that plants get nutrients from the soil, we get nutrients from food. Understanding where these nutrients come from and how they affect the body is what the science of nutrition is all about.

As soon as you take a bite of food or a sip of a drink, your body begins breaking it down into simpler substances through digestion. Digestion releases nutrients into the body. They are absorbed by the blood and carried to cells. Over the years, scientists have identified more than 50 different nutrients that are important for maintaining good health. These nutrients are usually placed into six main groups: **carbohydrates, fats, proteins,**

A tuna sandwich, milk, and fruit all contain sugar in the form of fructose, maltose, or lactose.

vitamins, minerals, and water. Let's take a look at the role that some of these nutrients play in the human body.

CARBOHYDRATES: ENERGY ENHANCERS

Most of the body's energy comes from carbohydrates. Carbohydrates get their name from the chemical elements that they contain: carbon, oxygen, and hydrogen. The three types of carbohydrates are **sugar, starch,** and **fiber.** When people hear the term *sugar*, they usually think of the white crystals that are added to drinks and foods to make them taste sweet. Table sugar, also called sucrose, is only one type of sugar. Fructose is a sugar found in most fruit, while maltose is found in grain, and lactose is in milk. All of these sugars are classified as simple carbohydrates because they have a simple chemical structure. On the other hand, starch is a complex carbohydrate. In **Experiment 3:** *Carbohydrate Starch Test*, you will have the opportunity to analyze several different foods to find out if they contain complex carbohydrates or not.

Carbohydrate Starch Test

Topic

How can you test for the presence of complex carbohydrates in different foods?

Introduction

Carbohydrates are one of the six categories of nutrients found in the food we eat. As carbohydrates are digested, they are converted into a simple sugar called glucose. Also known as blood sugar, glucose circulates throughout the body and acts as fuel for our cells. Carbohydrates can be either simple or complex. Sugars are simple carbohydrates that break down quickly during digestion, giving the body a quick burst of energy. Starch is a complex carbohydrate that is digested much more slowly. Because complex carbohydrates take longer to digest, they provide the body with energy over a much longer period of time. In this activity, you are going to test to see if starch is present in different food samples. You will use a solution of iodine. Normally, iodine is orange or red. When iodine encounters starch, it reacts and turns a deep, blue-black color.

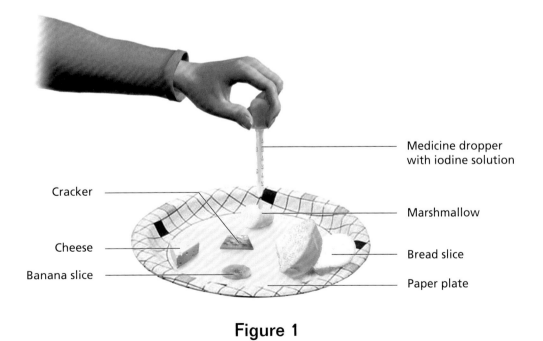

Cracker

Cheese

Banana slice

Medicine dropper
with iodine solution

Marshmallow

Bread slice

Paper plate

Figure 1

Time Required

45 minutes

Materials

- small bottle of Betadine® (10% iodine solution available in most pharmacies)
- medicine dropper
- large paper plates
- slice of raw potato
- slice of fresh banana
- marshmallow
- cracker
- shelled peanut, cashew, or similar large nut
- slice of bread
- small piece of cheese (Swiss or cheddar)
- slice of bologna, ham, turkey, or similar lunch meat
- safety glasses
- plastic garbage bag

Safety Note During this experiment, you will be using iodine solution as an indicator to test for the presence of starch in different types of food. Iodine is a potential poison and should not be taken internally. After testing the samples of food, dispose of them and the paper plate immediately. Always wear safety glasses when conducting the tests. The tests should be conducted under the guidance of a responsible adult. Please review and follow the safety guidelines before proceeding.

Procedure

1. Place each of the eight sample foods on the plate.
2. Place one drop of iodine solution on each sample of food. Wait 15 seconds. If the iodine turns a blue-black color, it means that there is starch

present in the food. If the iodine remains the same color, no starch is present.

3. Record the results of your tests on the data sheet. Throw away the food samples and paper plate in the garbage bag. If any iodine spills during the testing process, immediately clean it with a damp paper towel.

Data Table 1		
Food Sample	**Starch Present**	**No Reaction**
Banana		
Bread		
Cheese		
Cracker		
Lunch meat		
Marshmallow		
Nut		
Potato		

Analysis

1. Which of the food samples showed that starch was present?
2. What do all these food items have in common?
3. Based on your results, which of the following foods also should contain starch: rice, steak, tuna fish, butter, popcorn, or pasta?

 ## What's Going On?

Carbohydrates found in the foods we eat are our most important source of energy. Complex carbohydrates give us a steady supply of energy and keep blood sugar levels balanced. Eating enough complex carbohydrates also frees up proteins so that they can be used for building and repairing cells, rather than as a primary energy source. Nutritionists recommend that 55% to 65% of food calories should come from complex carbohydrates.

Almost all complex carbohydrates come from plant materials. Beans, potatoes, wheat, corn, rice, and oats—all are rich in starch. As a result, products made from these plants—such as pasta, bread, and cereals—also contain a high amount of starch. Over the years, carbohydrates have gotten a bad reputation as a fattening food. This is not always the case. If the body takes in more carbohydrates than it needs, then it stores the excess as fat. This often happens when we eat too many simple carbohydrates. These days, sugars are added to many foods and drinks. Because they break down quickly to form glucose in the blood, the body has to quickly store the excess. Complex carbohydrates break down more slowly, so they tend to be burned rather than stored. Of course eating too many calories from any source will lead to an increase in fat storage, but rather than eliminating carbohydrates, a better approach would be to eliminate excess sugar and replace it with complex carbohydrates.

Our Findings

1. The bread, cracker, potato, marshmallow, and banana should have tested positive for starch.
2. All of these food samples come from plants.
3. Rice, popcorn, and pasta all have starch in them.

FACTS ABOUT FIBER

One of the most important complex carbohydrates is dietary fiber. Fiber is the name that nutritionists use to describe the tough, stringy parts of fruits and vegetables. It forms the outer seed coat on grains such as rice, corn, and wheat. The body doesn't usually digest fiber. Instead, fiber passes through the digestive system, helping to move waste more efficiently. (You've probably noticed this if you eat a lot of corn on the cob.) Fiber helps to prevent constipation and may also provide long-term protection against certain types of cancer. Fiber-rich foods also fill you up without adding calories, so they are particularly important if you are trying to lose weight. The best way to increase the amount of fiber in your diet is to eat fruits and vegetables with edible skins and beans. In addition, breads and pasta made from whole-grain wheat, as well as brown rice, have much more fiber than processed white rice and bleached flour do.

PROTEINS: BUILDING BLOCKS FOR THE BODY

Proteins also contain calories. They can serve as a source of energy, but the main role of proteins in the human body is to

Steak and eggs are both high protein food sources. Protein maintains and replaces tissues in the human body. For example, protein is used to make hemoglobin, the part of red blood cells that carries oxygen to every part of your body.

build cells. Every cell is made of proteins, and because cells are continuously being replaced, new proteins from food are needed as long as a person is alive. The word *protein* comes from the ancient Greek term *proteins,* which means "of prime importance." Without a constant supply of new protein, the body would not be able to survive.

Proteins are made of long chains of molecules called **amino acids.** You can think of amino acids as being something like the letters in the alphabet. By combining different amino acids, your body can make hundreds of types of proteins. Proteins also are found in hormones, which help to control body systems, and enzymes, which control chemical reactions in the body. Many foods contain proteins, including meat, fish, milk, eggs, beans, and nuts. When you eat a food that is rich in protein, your body has to digest it to release the amino acids. In **Experiment 4: *Protein Digestion,*** you will discover how enzymes help break down proteins so that your body can make use of the amino acids that they contain.

EXPERIMENT 4 Protein Digestion

Topic

How do enzymes help the body digest proteins?

Introduction

Proteins are one of the six categories of nutrients that our bodies take in from the food we eat. The main role that proteins serve in the body is in building new cells. Proteins also are found in hormones and other body fluids. Proteins are made from complex molecules called amino acids. There are 22 different kinds of amino acids. Your body can manufacture 14 of them. The other eight are called essential amino acids, and they must come from the food you eat. In order to get these amino acids, your body must first digest the protein that you eat. This digestion is done with the help of special chemicals called enzymes. In this experiment, you will test to see how enzymes help to break down the proteins found in meat.

Time Required

45 minutes

Materials

- ½ lb (¼ kg) of raw chuck steak, or similar lower-grade cut of beef
- cutting board
- sharp kitchen knife
- 2 metal forks
- ½ teaspoon measure
- commercial meat tenderizer powder
- refrigerator
- plastic wrap
- 2 medium-sized plates

- barbeque grill, broiler, or large frying pan on a stove
- watch or timer

Safety Note During this experiment, you will be cooking a piece of meat and cutting it with a sharp knife. These activities should be conducted by and under the guidance of a responsible adult. Handling raw meat may lead to the transfer of bacteria. After cutting the meat, wash your hands and all surfaces with hot soapy water. Discard the meat after testing it. Do not eat it. Please review and follow the safety guidelines before proceeding.

Procedure

1. Have an adult use a sharp kitchen knife to cut the raw beef into two equal portions. Use a fork to place one piece of meat onto each plate. Have the adult carve an "X" on one piece of meat (Figure 1). Leave the other piece alone.

2. Sprinkle ½ teaspoon of meat tenderizer evenly across the top of the piece of meat with the "X" on it. Leave the other piece alone. Puncture the tops of both pieces of meat with the fork multiple times. Space the lines of holes about ¼ inch (½ cm) apart. Cover each piece of meat with plastic wrap and place them in the refrigerator for 30 minutes.

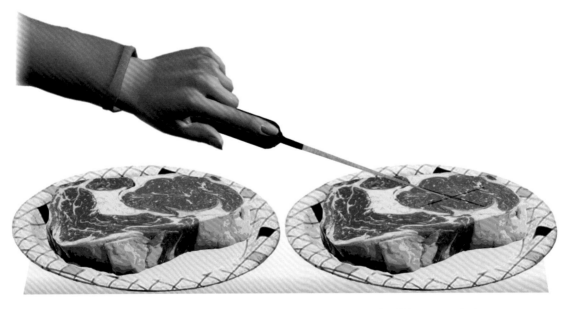

Second steak   Steak with "X" cut in it

Figure 1

3. After 30 minutes have passed, place the two pieces of meat side by side on the same grill or pan so that they cook with the same flame and for the same amount of time. Cook the meat for five minutes on one side. Use the fork to turn over the meat, and cook for another five minutes.

4. Place the meat back on the plates. Keep the piece that was treated with the tenderizer on the right side. Try tearing the meat apart by putting the tines of the two forks into each piece of meat and gently pulling in opposite directions. Compare the texture of the pieces of meat and the amount of effort needed to tear them.

Analysis

1. Why was it important that the two pieces of meat be cooked side by side for the same amount of time?

2. Which piece of meat was easier to tear apart with the fork after cooking?

3. How did the texture of the two pieces of meat compare with one another?

 ## What's Going On?

Meat and fish are high in protein and contain all the essential amino acids that a person needs in his or her diet. In order for these amino acids to be used by the body, however, protein must be broken down. This is done by chemicals called enzymes, which are found in the digestive system. Raw meat is usually quite tough and hard to tear because it contains a protein called collagen. Cooking a piece of meat will break down some of the proteins, making it easier to chew and digest. Commercial meat tenderizers contain enzymes, which react with the meat and "pre-digest" it. The longer a piece of meat is exposed to the action of these enzymes before cooking, the easier it will be to chew and digest.

Our Findings

1. In a controlled experiment, all of the variables must be the same except for the one that you are testing. In this experiment, all conditions have to be the same except that meat tenderizer was used on one of the pieces and not the other.

2. The piece of meat that was treated with the meat tenderizer was easier to pull apart.

3. The piece of meat that was not treated with the tenderizer was much tougher and had a stringy texture.

GOOD FAT, BAD FAT

These days, there is a great deal of discussion about how much fat should be in your diet. News reports and articles are constantly reminding us that fatty foods are bad for our health. In food stores, everything from milk and cereal to ice cream and cookies comes in low-fat varieties. Based on this information alone, you might think that eating anything with fat in it would be unhealthy.

However, not all fat is bad for you. In fact, like carbohydrates and protein, fat is one of the important nutrients that your body needs to survive. The scientific name for fat is **lipid.** All lipids are made from the elements carbon, hydrogen and oxygen, just like carbohydrates. The difference is in how the atoms of these elements are arranged. The main components of lipids are substances called fatty acids, which are attached to a chemical called glycerol. Fats are put into different groups based on the number of fatty acid molecules that are attached to the glycerol molecule. A triglyceride, for example, has three fatty acids (tri) attached to the glycerol.

Fats are further classified as being saturated or unsaturated, based on the number of hydrogen atoms attached to the carbon atoms in the fatty acids. A fat is saturated if there is a hydrogen atom attached to every available location on a carbon atom. Saturated fats generally are found in meats and the oils of certain plants, such as palm oil and coconut oil. Saturated fats are usually solid at room temperature. In an unsaturated fat, the carbon atoms could still link up with additional hydrogen atoms. Unsaturated fats include the oils of many plants, such as corn oil and olive oil. Unsaturated fats usually are liquids at room temperature.

Fat plays several important roles in your body. Like carbohydrates, fat provides your body with energy. Gram for gram, fats provide more than twice the number of calories (nine) as carbohydrates and proteins do (four). Fat also is needed to transport certain vitamins into your blood. When fats are digested, they break down into simpler materials called fatty acids. Your body can produce many of these substances, but it can't make them all. One example is linoleic acid, which is essential for maintaining proper growth and healthy skin. Because your body can't make linoleic acid, it must come from your diet.

Eating some fat is necessary for you to maintain good health, but eating too much saturated fat can cause health problems. Most meat contains saturated fat that you cannot even see. In **Experiment 5:** *Finding Hidden Fat in Meat*, you will test two different samples of beef to see just how much fat they contain.

EXPERIMENT 5

Finding Hidden Fat in Meat

Topic

How can you calculate how much hidden fat is found in meat?

Introduction

All meat contains some fat. In some cases you can see a layer of fat on top of the meat, such as on a chicken breast or on a steak. Trimming the fat with a knife will reduce the amount, but it won't get rid of it all. Even a so-called "lean" piece of meat has fat hidden in it. In this experiment, you will measure the amount of hidden fat found in two different samples of beef.

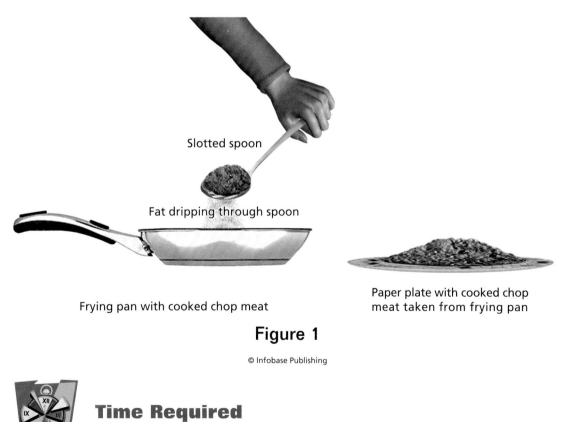

Slotted spoon

Fat dripping through spoon

Frying pan with cooked chop meat

Paper plate with cooked chop meat taken from frying pan

Figure 1

© Infobase Publishing

Time Required

60 minutes

Materials

- scale that is sensitive enough to weigh grams or $^1/_{10}$ of an ounce

- large frying pan

- stove or hot plate

- pot holder or oven mitt

- 2 large paper or Styrofoam hot cups

- 2 large paper plates

- large slotted spoon

- safety glasses

- ½ lb (¼ kg) ground beef—chuck variety labeled 75% lean

- ½ lb (¼ kg) ground beef—sirloin variety labeled 90% lean

- aluminum foil

- paper towels

- sink with hot, soapy water

- calculator

- adult to assist you

Safety Note This experiment should be conducted under the guidance of a responsible adult. During this experiment, you will be cooking meat on a stove to remove the fat. The frying pan and fat will be very hot. All cooking should be done by an adult. When pouring the hot, liquefied fat into the cups, the person should wear an oven mitt and safety glasses. Be careful not to spill any of the fat. Raw meat may contain bacteria and should be handled with care. After conducting the experiment, wash your hands and clean all the surfaces with hot soapy water. Dispose of the meat and cups containing fat in a suitable trash container. Please review and follow the safety guidelines before proceeding.

Procedure

1. Place each sample of ground beef on a separate piece of aluminum foil. Observe each sample, looking at the color and texture of the meat. Record your observations on the data table.

2. Use the aluminum foil to lift the sample of ground chuck (75% lean) and place it on the scale. Weigh the sample with the foil to the nearest $^1/_{10}$ oz (gram) and record it on the data sheet. Place the sample of meat in the frying pan. Spread the piece of aluminum foil on a paper plate. Heat the meat at a medium temperature. Use the spoon to break up any clumps of meat in the pan, and stir it every few minutes. After cooking for about 15 minutes, the meat in the pan should be completely browned. Use the slotted spoon to carefully transfer all of the browned meat from the pan to the foil-covered plate. When lifting the cooked meat, go slowly so that the fat drains through the slots in the spoon and stays in the frying pan.

3. Lift the cooked meat by the edges of the foil and place it on the scale. Weigh the meat and record the mass on the data table. Calculate the mass of the fat by subtracting the mass of the cooked meat from the mass of the raw meat. Divide the mass of the fat by the mass of the raw meat and multiply by 100. This will give you the percentage of fat found in the meat.

4. Carefully pour the liquid fat from the frying pan into one of the disposable cups and put it to the side to cool. Clean the frying pan with hot soapy water and dry it with a paper towel.

5. Repeat Steps 1 to 4 with the sample of ground sirloin (90% lean).

6. Observe the fat in the cups after it has been allowed to cool for about 30 minutes.

Data Table 1

Ground Chuck: 75% lean

Observations of raw meat: _____

_____

_____

Mass of raw sample _____ ounces (grams)

Mass of cooked sample after draining fat _____ ounces (grams)

Mass of fat (mass of raw sample – mass of cooked sample) _____ ounces (grams)

% fat in meat (mass of fat/mass of raw sample X 100) _____ %

Ground Sirloin: 90% lean

Observations of raw meat: _____

_____

_____

Mass of raw sample _____ ounces (grams)

Mass of cooked sample after draining fat _____ ounces (grams)

Mass of fat (mass of raw sample – mass of cooked sample) _____ ounces (grams)

% fat in meat (mass of fat/mass of raw sample X 100) _____ %

Analysis

1. How did the color and texture of the two meat samples appear before you cooked them?
2. What happened to the fat in the meat as you began to heat it?
3. Which sample of meat produced the greatest percentage of fat?
4. What happened to the fat in the cups after it was allowed to cool?

 ## What's Going On?

No meat is 100% fat free. Even the leanest cut of meat has some fat in it. In this experiment, you compared the fat levels in two varieties of beef. Sirloin is a relatively lean cut of meat, but it still has a high percentage of fat hidden in it. This hidden fat is known as marbling; it is what gives the meat its flavor and texture. If all of the fat were removed from the meat, it would be very dry and have little taste. When meat is cooked, the fat in it begins to melt and turn into a liquid. This process is called rendering. When the liquefied fat is captured and cooled, it is turned into a fatty product called tallow. In the past, tallow was used to make candles and soap, and it was used as a lubricant. It was also used to fry foods. Because it is made from animal fat, tallow is extremely high in saturated fat. Instead of cooking with tallow, many people and restaurants use vegetable oil. Vegetable oil contains unsaturated fat, which is considered to be much healthier.

Our Findings

1. The two samples looked very similar although the chuck may have been slightly paler in color. It is difficult to see the fat in either sample of meat.
2. As the meat was heated, the fat liquefied.
3. The ground chuck has a higher percentage of fat than the ground sirloin.
4. After the fat in the cups cooled, it turned into a white solid.

A WORD ABOUT CHOLESTEROL

When people are discussing the effects of eating fats in foods, they often use the term *cholesterol*. Cholesterol is not a true fat. It is a waxy, fatlike substance found in every cell membrane in your body. In most cases, your cells and liver produce all the cholesterol that your body needs; it is not required in the diet. Cholesterol travels from the liver through the blood by special chemicals called lipoproteins. These molecules come in two main varieties. High-density lipoprotein (HDL), also known as "good cholesterol," helps to keep your blood vessels clear of fat deposits and working efficiently. Low-density lipoprotein (LDL), the so-called "bad cholesterol," tends to clog arteries. LDL is a bulky molecule that can create a variety of health problems. LDL is found in many meats, eggs and dairy products, such as cheese and ice cream. For this reason, health experts recommend limiting these foods in the diet. They suggest eating more fresh fruit and whole grains, which are high in HDL cholesterol.

VITAMINS AND MINERALS

Vitamins and minerals are not needed in the same quantities as carbohydrates, proteins, and fats, but they are just as important for maintaining good health. Vitamins work with enzymes to help control chemical changes in the body. Vitamins usually are separated into two groups. Water-soluble vitamins are found in many fruits and vegetables; they include vitamins C and B. As the name suggests, these vitamins are carried into the digestive system dissolved in water. Most fruit juices are high in these vitamins. If you cook fruits and vegetables in water for a long time and then dispose of the water, you have lost many of the vitamins. Fat-soluble vitamins include vitamins A, D, E, and K. These vitamins are found in meats and oils.

Minerals are the building blocks of rocks, and many are also essential elements for living things. They come from soil and are passed up food chains until they enter our bodies. Iron is a mineral that is a component of red blood cells. Calcium is used to make bone. Phosphorus helps to regulate blood chemistry.

Vitamins and Minerals

Water-Soluble Vitamins:

Vitamin	Role in the Body	Food Source
C	Protects against infection, formation of connective tissue, helps wounds heal, keeps blood vessels strong	Citrus fruits, broccoli, cabbage, tomatoes
B1	Changes glucose into fat, promotes a good appetite	Whole grain cereals, liver, nuts, wheat germ, legumes
B2	Essential for the metabolism of fats, carbohydrates, and proteins, keeps skin healthy.	Leafy green vegetables, milk, cheese, eggs, fish
Niacin	Needed by body in energy production, to use carbohydrates, to synthesize fat, and for tissue respiration. Important for the maintenance of body tissues.	Yeast, liver, eggs, fish, wheat germ.
B	Essential for amino acid and carbohydrate metabolism.	Wheat bran and germ, liver, meat, fish, whole grains
Folic Acid	Necessary for the production of RNA and DNA and normal red blood cells.	Liver, nuts, green vegetables, orange juice
B12	Necessary for the production of red blood cells and normal growth.	Meat, liver, eggs, milk

Fat-Soluble Vitamins:

Vitamin	Role in the Body	Food Source
A	Growth of body cells, strengthens teeth, utilization of calcium and phosphorus in bone formation, keeps eyes moist	Milk and other dairy products green vegetables, carrots
D	Essential for normal bone and tooth development	Fish oils, beef, butter, eggs, milk, also produced by skin with exposure to sunlight
E	Protects against red blood cell destruction	Yellow vegetable oils and wheat germ
K	Shortens blood-clotting time	Spinach, eggs, liver, cabbage, tomatoes.

Minerals:		
Calcium	Building material for bones and teeth, heart muscle contraction, blood clotting	Dairy products, leafy vegetables, apricots
Phosphorus	Combines with calcium to make bones strong, essential for cell metabolism, keeps blood pH balanced.	Peas, beans, milk, broccoli, meat, cottage cheese
Iron	Part of red blood cell's oxygen transport system, important for resistance to infection, necessary for cellular respiration	Liver, red meat, shellfish, peanuts, dried fruit, eggs
Iodine	Essential component of thyroid hormone, thyroxine; maintains proper water balance	Iodized salt, seafood
Manganese	Enzyme activator for carbohydrate, protein and fat metabolism; important for the growth of cartilage and bone tissue	Wheat germ, nuts, bran, green leafy vegetables, cereal grains
Copper	An essential part of several respiratory enzymes; needed for the development of young red blood cells	Liver, beans, Brazil nuts, whole meal flour, lentils
Zinc	Essential component of insulin and many enzyme systems.	Shellfish, meat, milk, eggs
Fluorine	Essential for normal tooth and bone growth	Toothpaste and treated water
Molybdenum	Essential for enzymes that make uric acid	Legumes and meat products
Sodium	Regulates fluid balance in body	Table salt, beans, beets, dried apricots, spinach, raisins
Chloride	Part of digestive juice in stomach and saliva	Table salt, beans, beets, dried apricots, spinach, raisins
Potassium	Helps to control pH and fluid balance, enzyme activator in the use of amino acids	Most foods
Magnesium	Enzyme activator for carbohydrate metabolism	Most foods
Sulfur	Component of insulin and amino acids builds hair, skin and nails	Nuts, dried fruits, barley, oatmeal, eggs, beans, cheese

MAKING WISE FOOD CHOICES

Today, people have a wide range of food choices. A healthy diet includes all of the necessary nutrients. To maintain a proper weight, it is important to limit the total amount of calories that you take in each day. The U.S. government passed a law requiring that the makers of pre-packaged foods list all the ingredients used in the production of the food. In addition, each product must carry a label that provides a detailed breakdown of the calories and the nutrients found in the food. In **Experiment 6: *Reading Food Labels***, you will see how several common foods "stack up" against each other when it comes to providing you with the nutrients you need each day.

Topic

What type of information is found on nutritional information labels?

Introduction

In the United States, all packaged foods are required to have a label that lists a variety of information, including the recommended serving size,

Nutrition Facts

Serving Size 1cup (228g)
Servings Per Container 2

Amount Per Serving

Calories 250   Calories from fat 110

% Daily Value*

Total Fat 12g	**18%**
Saturated Fat 3g	**15%**
Trans Fat 3g	
Cholesterol 30g	**10%**
Sodium 470mg	**20%**
Total Carbohydrate 31g	**10%**
Dietary Fiber 0g	**0%**
Sugars 5g	
Protein 5g	

Vitamin A	4%
Vitamin C	2%
Calcium	20%
Iron	4%

*Percent Daily Values are based on a 2,000 calorie diet. Your Daily Values may be higher or lower depending on your calorie needs.

	Calories:	2,000	2,500
Total Fat	Less than	65g	80g
Sat Fat	Less than	20g	25g
Cholesterol	Less than	300mg	300mg
Sodium	Less than	2,400mg	2,400mg
Total Carbohydrate		300g	375g
Dietary Fiber		25g	30g

Figure 1

the calories per serving, the number of calories coming from fat, and the vitamins and minerals that the food contains. The label also must list the amounts of fat, protein, carbohydrates, sugars, sodium, fiber, and cholesterol found in the food. These nutrients are listed two ways: by their weight in grams and by their Percent Daily Values. The Percent Daily Value shows what percentage one serving of the product satisfies a person's daily need of that nutrient. The percentage is usually based on a 2,000-calorie per day diet. In this activity, you will compare the nutritional labels of several packaged foods to see which combination provides all the nutrients you would need on a single day.

Time Required

60 minutes

Materials

- can of tuna fish in water
- natural cheese (not processed American cheese food)
- container of low-fat milk
- box of Frosted Flakes or similar sweetened cereal
- container of plain old-fashioned or traditional oatmeal
- 12-oz (355-mL) can of regular cola (not diet)

Safety Note No special safety precautions are needed for this activity. Please review and follow the safety guidelines before proceeding.

Procedure

1. Find the nutritional label on each food package. Use the information found on the labels to fill in the data table and answer the questions.

Data Table 1						
	Tuna	**Oatmeal**	**Cereal**	**Milk**	**Cheese**	**Soda**
Serving size						
Calories per serving						
Calories from fat						
Saturated fat						
Total fat						
Sodium						
Total carbohydrates						
Sugars						
Other carbohydrates						
Dietary Fiber						
Protein						

Analysis

1. Which food products contain the most protein per serving?
2. Which products have high levels of saturated fat?

3. Which product provided the most dietary fiber?

4. Which product contained the lowest amount of fat?

5. Which product had the highest amount of sodium?

6. Based on the labels, which food product would be least nutritious?

 What's Going On?

Different foods contain different amounts of nutrients. Nutritional fact labels help a person make wise choices when it comes to the foods they eat. Many foods can provide a person with the calories they need to survive, but how those calories are delivered can vary. Good sources of calories are complex carbohydrates and unsaturated fats. These take longer to digest, so they make you feel full longer. Because proteins are needed for the growth and repair of cells, you also need to eat foods that contain protein.

Avoid foods high in sodium, sugar, and saturated fat. For example, soft drinks are high in calories, but almost all of the calories come from simple sugars. These have a very low nutritional value. Sweetened cereals contain some complex carbohydrates, but they also are high in sugar and sodium. In fact, most processed foods contain higher levels of sodium and sugar than fresh foods do. One way to avoid this problem is to eat fresh fruits and vegetables and whole-grain cereals and breads as much as possible.

Our Findings

1. Tuna, milk, and cheese are all high in protein

2. Milk and cheese are high in saturated fat.

3. The oatmeal had the most fiber.

4. The soda had the lowest amount of fat.

5. Answers will vary, but the tuna and cheese usually have high amounts of sodium.

6. The soda would be the least nutritious because it provides calories only from processed sugar.

WATER: THE ELIXIR OF LIFE

Though water has no calories, it often is considered the most important nutrient. About two-thirds of your body weight is water. Water is found in every human cell and helps to regulate almost every body function. Most of your blood is made of water, and water allows you to digest food and eliminate waste. Many foods contain water, but it also is important to drink about ½ gallon (2 L) of water each day to keep your body hydrated.

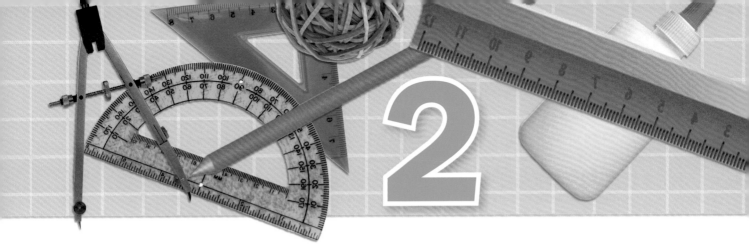

2

The Chemistry of Food

When people hear the word *chemistry*, they often picture scientists in white lab coats working in a lab with a lot of high-tech equipment to mix complex formulas. Even though it might not look like it, a chef working in a kitchen uses almost as much chemistry as a scientist working in a lab. Chemistry is the branch of science that explores matter and the way it changes. Food is nothing more than matter. **Matter** is defined as any substance that has mass and takes up space. Matter comes in several different states, including solid, liquid, and gas, and it can change in two ways.

Chefs are like scientists, using chemical properties to create meals.

PHYSICAL CHANGES IN FOOD

When matter undergoes a **physical change**, the chemical make-up of the substance remains constant. Examples of physical changes include water turning into ice, or rocks breaking apart. Food undergoes many types of physical change. When ice cream melts, it makes a physical change because it can be frozen again. When vegetables are cut up, they are still vegetables; only the size and shape have changed. In **Experiment 7: Dehydrated Fruit**, you will test to see what happens to fruit when the water is removed and then put back again.

EXPERIMENT 7

Dehydrated Fruit

Topic

How much water is contained in different types of fruit?

Introduction

Every type of fresh fruit has water in it. The process in which water is removed from a piece of fruit is called dehydration. This is one example of a physical change that food undergoes. Unlike chemical changes, physical changes can usually be reversed. In this activity, you will test to see if the dehydration of fruit is truly a physical change and, in the process, determine how much water different types of fruit normally store.

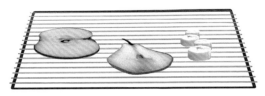

Oven rack

Figure 1

© Infobase Publishing

Time Required

30 minutes for preparation and measurement, 4 hours for drying

Materials

- scale
- standard oven or convection oven
- 3 pieces of clean metal screen, each about 6 in. x 12 in. (15 cm x 30 cm)
- fresh banana
- fresh apple
- fresh pear

- cutting board

- sharp knife

- oven mitt

- spatula

- 3 large paper plates

- marker

- watch or timer

- large bowl of water

- calculator

- adult to assist you

Safety Note   This experiment should be conducted under the guidance of a responsible adult. During this experiment, you will be slicing fruit and drying it in an oven. Please review and follow the safety guidelines before proceeding.

Procedure

1. Use the marker to label the three paper plates "banana," "apple," and "pear."

2. Peel the banana and place it on the cutting board. Cut the banana across the length so that the slices are about ½ in. (1 cm) wide. Observe the banana slices and record how they look and feel. Place the sliced banana on its plate and weigh it on the scale. Record the weight on the data table under the heading "Wet Weight." Place the slices of banana on one of the metal screens and put it off to the side.

3. Place the apple on the cutting board on its side. Using the knife, slice the apple horizontally, starting from the bottom of the fruit so that each slice is about ½ in. (1 cm) wide. Place the apple slices on the plate marked "apple." Weigh and record as you did with the banana. Transfer the apple slices onto the second metal screen.

4. Repeat Step 3 with the pear.

5. Turn the oven to 200˚F (93˚C) and place all three screens on oven racks at the same time. Heat the fruit for four hours. Then turn the oven off and remove the screens. Use the spatula to remove the banana slices and place them back on their plate. Look at the banana slices and record your

observations on the data table. Weigh the plate on the scale and record it on the data table under the heading "Dry weight." Repeat the same procedure with the apple slices and pear slices.

6. Calculate the percent water weight in each piece of fruit using the following method: Subtract the dry weight from the wet weight to get the water weight. Divide the water weight by the wet weight and multiply by 100.

7. After you have finished your calculations, take one slice of each piece of fruit and place it in a bowl of water for about 15 minutes. Remove the fruit and observe it. Compare it to the dried fruit slices; if you wish, taste a slice of each. Record your observations on the data tables.

Data Table 1	
Observations of Fresh Fruit	
Banana	
Apple	
Pear	

Data Table 2
Weight Calculations for the Banana
Wet weight: _____ ounces (oz) or grams (g)
Dry weight: _____ oz or g
Water weight: (wet weight – dry weight) _____ oz or g
% Water: (water weight/wet weight x 100) _____

Data Table 3
Weight Calculations for the Apple
Wet weight: _____ oz or g

Dry weight: _____ oz or g
Water weight: (wet weight – dry weight) _____ oz or g
% Water: (water weight/wet weight x 100) _____

Data Table 4
Weight Calculations for the Pear
Wet weight: _____ oz or g
Dry weight: _____ oz or g
Water weight: (wet weight – dry weight) _____ oz or g
% Water: (water weight/wet weight x 100) _____

Data Table 5	
Observations of Dry Fruit	
Banana	
Apple	
Pear	

Data Table 6	
Observations of Rehydrated Fruit	
Banana	
Apple	
Pear	

Analysis

1. What was the texture of the fruit slices before they were placed in the oven?
2. How did the color and texture change after the fruit was removed from the oven?
3. What happened to the texture of the fruit slices that were placed in the bowl of water after they were heated?
4. Which type of fruit contained the highest percentage of water?

What's Going On?

Water is an essential nutrient for all living things. Many of the foods we eat contain a large amount of water. This is especially true of fruits and vegetables. In this experiment you "dehydrated" the fruit by heating it in an oven. Heating the fruit causes some of the water contained in the cells to evaporate. As the water is removed, the weight of the fruit decreases. Because water is being removed from cells, they tend to collapse. This makes the fruit wrinkled and harder. Placing pieces of dried fruit in water will partially rehydrate them. They will swell, but usually will not gain back all the water they lost.

In this experiment, you compared the water content of three fruits by removing the water and comparing the weight loss. Because you dried the fruit for only a few hours, you did not remove all the water. This would have required several days of drying. If you could remove all the water from these fruits, you would find that both apples and pears contain about 84% water. Bananas are about 74% water. As you might have guessed, watermelon has one of the highest water contents. A typical watermelon is about 92% water.

Our Findings

1. The apple and pear were both firm and wet, while the banana was soft and mushy.
2. All of the fruit was harder and wrinkled after drying.
3. When the fruit slices were placed in the water again, they became soft and swelled up.
4. The apple and pear should have contained more water, and the banana less water.

JERKY, RAISINS, AND PRUNES

When food is full of moisture, it makes an ideal habitat in which bacteria and mold can live and multiply. Because of this, when food is full of moisture, it spoils rather quickly and must be discarded. Thousands of years ago, people discovered that drying food would make it last much longer. Dehydration was one of the first methods of food preservation. Native Americans used dehydration to make pemmican. This high-protein snack was made from dried meat (usually deer or buffalo), animal fat, and dried berries. Drying the meat not only preserved it but also made it much lighter to carry. Today, when people go on long hikes and camping trips, they often take dehydrated food with them, such as raisins, prunes, and dried strips of meat called jerky.

CHEMICAL CHANGES IN FOOD

A **chemical change** is one in which the molecular structure of the substance is permanently altered. Unlike a physical change, a chemical change usually cannot be reversed. Chemical changes are very common in food. When you grill a piece of meat or boil an egg, chemical changes happen. Once the meat or egg is cooked, you can't "un-cook" it. Heating food is only one way to bring about a chemical change. In **Experiment 8: *Chemical Changes Involved in Making Cheese,*** you will test a different type of chemical change. In this case, you will use an **acid** to cause a chemical reaction in milk to make a simple type of cheese.

EXPERIMENT 8

Chemical Changes Involved in Making Cheese

Topic

How is a chemical change used to make cheese?

Introduction

"Little Miss Muffet sat on a tuffet, eating her curds and whey...." Most people are familiar with this classic nursery rhyme, but they may not know what "curds and whey" are. This traditional English dish is similar to cottage cheese. It is made using vinegar, which creates a chemical reaction with milk. In this activity, you will have the opportunity to use some kitchen chemistry to make a bowl of curds and whey and discover how a simple chemical change can be put to practical use.

Bowl of milk mixture

Strainer

Figure 1

Time Required

45 minutes

Materials

- 2 clean glass or stainless-steel mixing bowls
- 2 cups (500 mL) fresh, fat-free (skim) milk at room temperature
- ¼ cup (50 mL) white vinegar
- timer or watch
- large wooden spoon
- clear plastic wrap
- paper plate
- clean strainer with a fine mesh opening

Safety Note No special safety precautions are needed for this activity. Please review and follow the safety guidelines before proceeding.

Procedure

1. Pour the milk into one of the mixing bowls and allow it to warm to room temperature.
2. Gently stir the white vinegar into the milk, observing the milk as you do. Cover the bowl with clear plastic wrap and allow it to stand undisturbed for 10 minutes. Record your observations.
3. After 10 minutes have elapsed, remove the plastic wrap and observe the milk. Hold the strainer over the second bowl and pour the milk mixture through the strainer, capturing all the liquid in the second bowl. Rinse the material that was trapped in the strainer under cold water for about 15 seconds.
4. After rinsing and draining, empty the material that was trapped in the strainer onto the paper plate and observe its texture. If you wish, sample a small amount to see how it tastes. Record your observations.

Analysis

1. What happened to the milk when you first poured in the vinegar and stirred it gently?

2. How did the texture of the milk change after it was allowed to stand for 10 minutes?

3. After you strained the milk mixture, what was the texture of the material left in the strainer?

4. How did the material trapped in the strainer taste after rinsing it?

 ## What's Going On?

Milk contains a protein called casein. Vinegar is a form of acid known as acetic acid. When the casein in milk is mixed with acid, a chemical reaction takes place and the protein forms a solid. This process is called coagulation. It causes clumps which are commonly known as curds, to form in the milk. The whey, which is mostly water, is the liquid that is left behind. When the curds are separated from the whey, they can be used to make a variety of different cheeses. As with many chemical reactions, the coagulation of casein happens faster if the milk is warm. Heating the milk to a temperature of about 122°F (50°C) before adding the vinegar causes the casein to coagulate almost immediately.

Our Findings

1. Small solid clumps started to form in the milk.

2. The milk curdled and separated into white chunks (curds) and a clear liquid (whey).

3. The solid curds had a light rubbery texture.

4. The curds had a slightly sour taste.

ACIDS IN THE KITCHEN

People often think of acids as toxic chemicals that can cause severe burns and corrode metal. Some acids are extremely dangerous, but others are harmless. Acids are frequently found in foods and drinks. As we saw in the previous experiment, vinegar is really acetic acid. Orange juice, lemonade, and tomato juice all contain citric acid, and yogurt contains lactic acid. The word *acid* comes from the Latin term *acidus*, which means "sour." Acids do usually taste sour. Acids have many uses in the kitchen, from making cheese to preserving foods by pickling them. In **Experiment 9:** *Marinating Meat and Bones*, you will discover another important use of acid in the food preparation process.

Marinating Meat and Bones

Topic

How does an acid marinade affect the properties of meat and bone?

Introduction

One popular way to prepare a piece of chicken, meat, or fish for grilling is to marinate it first by soaking it in a solution of spices and a liquid, such as vinegar or wine. Marinating not only adds flavor but also causes several chemical changes that affect the food's texture. In this activity, you will discover some of the chemical changes that happen to meat and bone when they are marinated in vinegar for an extended period of time.

Clean chicken bone

White vinegar "covering" bone

Figure 1

Time Required

20 minutes preparation, 5 days for completion and observation

Materials

- small glass baking dish
- small (16-oz) glass jar with lid
- white vinegar
- chicken leg bone with all the meat removed
- ½ lb (¼ kg) piece of raw, skinless chicken breast
- sink
- refrigerator
- clear plastic wrap
- latex exam gloves
- 2 metal forks
- 2 large zipper-style plastic bags
- adult to assist you

Safety Note Always wear gloves when handling the raw chicken and bones. Wash your hands and all surfaces with warm, soapy water after completing the experiment because raw meat and bones may contain harmful bacteria. This activity should be conducted under the guidance of a responsible adult. Please review and follow the safety guidelines before proceeding.

Procedure

1. Place the raw chicken breast in the glass dish. Observe the color. Using the two forks, poke it a few times to test the firmness and texture. Use the forks to try to pull the meat apart. Record your observations on the data chart. Pour white vinegar into the dish until it completely covers the chicken breast. Cover the dish with clear plastic wrap and place it in the refrigerator in a safe location. Allow it to stand for 24 hours.

2. Put on the exam gloves and hold the chicken bone in your hands. Observe its color and feel its texture. Try bending the bone to see how strong it is. Record your observations on the data chart and place the bone in the glass jar. Fill the jar with white vinegar and screw the lid on tight. Place the jar in a safe location for 24 hours. The jar with the bone does not have to be refrigerated.

3. After 24 hours have passed, retrieve the dish with the chicken breast from the refrigerator and remove the plastic wrap from the dish. Observe the color and texture of the meat. Use the two forks to probe the meat as you did in Step 1, and record your observations on the data table. After you have made your observations, use a fork to place the chicken breast into the plastic bag and zip it closed. Throw the bag with the chicken breast in the trash and pour the remaining vinegar down the sink drain. Wash the dish in hot soapy water.

4. Retrieve the jar with the chicken bone. While wearing rubber gloves, carefully remove the bone from the jar with the vinegar. Observe the bone closely and try bending it again. Record your observations on the data table. Return the bone to the jar for another 24 hours.

5. Repeat Step 4 with the chicken bone, making certain to record your data on the table. Follow this same procedure for two more days, until you have observed the chicken bone for five days. After you have completed the last observations, pour the vinegar from the jar down the drain while running cold water to dilute it. Place the chicken bone into a plastic bag and zip it closed. Dispose of the bag in the trash. Wash the glass jar with hot, soapy water.

	Data Table 1				
	Initial Observations	Day 2 Observations	Day 3 Observations	Day 4 Observations	Day 5 Observations
Chicken breast					
Chicken bone					

Analysis

1. How did the chicken breast appear before it was placed in the vinegar?

2. How did the chicken bone feel before it was placed in the vinegar?

3. What changes happened to the chicken breast after it soaked in the vinegar for 24 hours?

4. How did the chicken bone change over the course of five days?

5. Based on this experiment, what is the purpose of marinating meat in acid solutions before cooking it?

 ## What's Going On?

When people eat steak, chicken breast, or pot roast, they are eating animal muscle tissue. This tissue is made from several proteins, which in many cases are quite tough. In order to help soften the meat before cooking, many recipes call for the meat to be marinated in solutions that include wine or vinegar. Both of these substances are acids. Exposure to acid brings about a chemical change in proteins that helps to break down some of the protein fibers. This makes the meat easier to cut and chew.

Because marinades penetrate only a shallow depth into a cut of meat, they usually work best on thin cuts of meat or on meat that has been sliced or diced. Marinades take longer to work on meats that are dense, such as beef and pork. Chicken breast and most fish have more delicate muscle fibers, so they break down faster. As a result, these types of meat should be marinated for only a short time. Otherwise, the surface of the meat will dry out and become tough; it will almost appear to have been cooked. This is what happened to the chicken breast in this experiment.

Bone is also made of protein, with a solid matrix of a chemical known as calcium phosphate. The calcium phosphate makes the bone hard. When bone is placed in an acid solution, the calcium phosphate dissolves, leaving the proteins behind. As a result, the bone has a rubbery texture and can bend and twist.

Our Findings

1. The chicken breast was pinkish in color, and the meat was tough. It was difficult to pull the meat apart with the forks.

2. The chicken bone was hard and difficult to bend.

3. After 24 hours, the chicken breast turned white, and it was much easier to separate the meat with the forks.

4. After five days, the chicken bone became rubbery and could bend easily.

5. Marinating meat before cooking it makes the meat more tender, but marinating for too long can dry a piece of meat out and make it look cooked even before it is heated.

COOKING CAN BE A GAS

When a chemical reaction takes place, one common result is that it will produce a new substance that has a different state of matter from the original materials. In **Experiment 8: *Chemical Changes Involved in Making Cheese***, you started with milk and vinegar, which are both liquids. When mixed, they reacted to produce curds, which are a solid. In **Experiment 2: *Measuring Energy Stored in Foods***, you burned a marshmallow. As the marshmallow burned, a chemical change took place, releasing a large amount of smoke. The smoke contained carbon dioxide, which is a gas. There are a number of ways that gases can be produced during the preparation and cooking of food. In **Experiment 10: *Making Gas***, you will test several common kitchen substances to see which can be used to make a gas and how that gas can be put to use.

EXPERIMENT 10

Making Gas

Topic

Which kitchen substances commonly produce a gas when mixed together?

Introduction

Of the three common states of matter, a gas is the most difficult to detect. In most cases, you cannot see a gas, and unless the gas is in motion, you usually cannot feel it. The one time a gas is easily detected is when it is filling a container, such as a balloon or a bag, or when it is mixed in a liquid. If you blow into a straw in a glass of water or milk, you see air bubbles moving through the liquid. In this activity, you will use this property of a gas to see which combinations of cooking chemicals react to produce a gas.

Time Required

45 minutes

Materials

- baking soda
- baking powder
- white baking flour
- white vinegar
- warm water
- teaspoon
- 6 large (16-oz) clear plastic cups
- 6 small (3-oz) plastic cups
- permanent marker
- paper towels

> **Safety Note** No special safety precautions are needed for this activity. Please review and follow the safety guidelines before proceeding.

Procedure

1. Use the marker to label the six large plastic cups as follows: "vinegar and flour," "water and flour," "vinegar and baking soda," "water and baking soda," "vinegar and baking powder," and "water and baking powder." When you are finished, it should look like Figure 1. Then label three of the smaller cups "vinegar" and the other three cups "water."

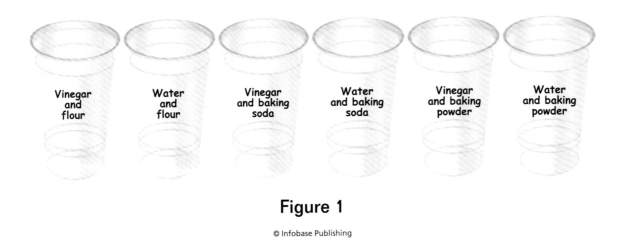

Figure 1

© Infobase Publishing

2. Put two level teaspoons of flour in each of the two cups with "flour" on the label. Clean the spoon with a paper towel and put two level teaspoons of baking soda in each of the two cups with "baking soda" on the label. Clean the spoon again and put two level teaspoons of baking powder in each of the two cups with "baking powder" on the label.

3. Fill the three smaller cups labeled "vinegar" with vinegar and the three cups labeled "water" with warm water.

4. Slowly pour one of the cups labeled "water" into the large cup labeled "water and flour." Wait one minute for a reaction to take place, and then record your observations. Do the same with the other two cups of water and the baking soda and baking powder. Repeat the procedure with the three cups of vinegar. Record your observations of each mixture.

Analysis

1. What happened when you added the vinegar to the baking soda? How did this compare to adding the vinegar to the baking powder?

2. What happened when you mixed the water with the baking soda? How did this compare to adding the water to the baking powder?

3. How did you know if a mixture caused a chemical reaction to produce a gas?

4. Which of the three powders did not have a chemical reaction when mixed with a liquid?

What's Going On?

In this activity, you tested three different powders commonly used in baking bread and cakes. Baking soda is a chemical called sodium bicarbonate. It is classified as a **base**. A base is the chemical opposite of an acid. Vinegar is an acid. Water is neither an acid nor a base. It is considered to be chemically neutral.

When an acid and a base are mixed together, they react to form a salt, and often a gas is released. Baking powder is a chemical mixture that contains both sodium bicarbonate and an acid, such as cream of tartar, monocalcium phosphate, or both. When baking powder is mixed with water, the acid and base react to form carbon dioxide gas. However, when baking powder is mixed with an acid, such as vinegar, little or no reaction happens because the solution has too much acid in it. Flour is chemically neutral, so it doesn't react with either vinegar or water.

Our Findings

1. When the vinegar was added to the baking soda, it immediately started to bubble. There was little or no reaction when the vinegar was added to the baking powder.

2. When the water was mixed with the baking powder, it reacted slowly, but bubbles did appear. There was no reaction between the water and baking soda.

3. You can tell that a gas was produced when the mixture started bubbling.

4. The flour did not react with either liquid.

BUBBLES, BAGELS, AND BEER

Carbon dioxide gas plays an important role in many of the foods that people consume each day. Beverages such as soda, beer, and champagne all get their "fizz" from carbon dioxide gas. The holes in Swiss cheese also are formed by carbon dioxide gas, released by bacteria during the curing process. The most common place where carbon dioxide bubbles make their appearance in food is in bread. If you look at a piece of bread, you can see that it is full of holes. **Yeast** are tiny organisms that are a common component of bread dough. As you will later discover, yeast release carbon dioxide gas when they eat. This makes the dough rise, and it also makes tiny holes in the baked bread.

As you discovered in the previous experiments, yeast and bacteria aren't the only ways that carbon dioxide bubbles get into food. Often, baking powder or baking soda is added to cake batter. These chemicals work much faster than yeast and are particularly effective in batter, which is much more liquid than bread dough. Whether it's from yeast, bacteria, or chemical compounds, a little carbon dioxide gas goes a long way in making foods lighter and fluffier.

Carbon dioxide caused by yeast fermentation causes holes to form in baked bread. The holes are produced when the air isn't properly pressed out of the dough when the loaves are shaped or when the dough is left to rise too long before baking.

The Heat Is On (and Off!)

When it comes to preparing food, one of the most important steps usually involves **heat.** Whether you fry an egg, grill a steak, or bake a cake, if it were not for the addition of heat, your food wouldn't get cooked. When people make ice cream, they must remove heat energy in order to make it freeze. While this sounds simple enough, the way that heat moves from one place to another can get pretty complicated. Before we can discuss some of the ways that heat affects different foods, we must first look at what heat is and how it behaves.

All matter is made up of molecules in constant motion, vibrating back and forth. This motion is called thermal energy. The greater the amount of motion, the greater the amount of thermal energy an object has. We measure the amount of thermal energy in a substance by taking its **temperature.** The greater the amount of molecular motion, the hotter an object is. You can think of heat as the amount of thermal energy transferred from one substance to another because of a difference in temperature between them.

When you boil water in a tea kettle, you add heat and increase the amount of thermal energy in the water. The water molecules begin vibrating faster and the temperature rises. Eventually, the water in the kettle gains so much thermal energy that it changes from a liquid to a gas. The opposite happens when you make ice. When you put water in a freezer, you are removing heat and decreasing the amount of thermal energy found in the water. The temperature of the water decreases until it loses so much thermal energy that it turns solid.

One of the most important rules regarding heat is that it always travels from things that are warmer to things that are colder. This rule is so important that it is referred to as the second law of thermodynamics. When two objects with different temperatures are brought in contact with each other, the warmer one will get cooler and the cooler one will get warmer until the two temperatures balance. If you hold an ice cube in your hand, it feels cold because the heat travels from your hand to the ice. When you hold a hot cup of tea or cocoa, the heat travels from the cup to your hand. Heat can move by **conduction, convection,** and **radiation. In Experiment 11:** *How Water Heats,* you will test these three ways of transferring heat by seeing which is the most efficient at heating a cup of water.

How Water Heats

Topic

Which form of heat transfer is most efficient at heating water?

Introduction

The second law of thermodynamics states that heat travels from a warmer substance to a colder substance. There are three ways in which this can happen. If you place the end of a metal rod in a fire, the entire rod will eventually become too hot to handle. The heat travels up the rod from the end that is in the fire by a process called conduction. Conduction usually happens in solids, and it is the result of rapidly vibrating molecules coming into direct contact with one another.

In liquids and gases, the main form of heat transfer is called convection. During convection, heat moves through a fluid by means of currents. As a fluid gets hot, it expands and becomes less dense. This makes it rise away from the heat source. As the fluid moves out, it begins to cool again and becomes denser. This causes it to sink, setting up a circular flow of heat through the fluid called a convection cell.

Thermometer

Measuring cup with water

Figure 1

Radiation is the third form of heat transfer. With radiation, heat is transferred by means of waves or pulses of energy that are created by rapidly vibrating electrons found in energized molecules. If you stand in bright sunlight, you will feel warm because radiation from the sun strikes your body and is absorbed by your skin.

In this activity, you will test to see which form of heat transfer is most efficient at heating a cup of water.

Time Required

45 minutes

Materials

- 2-cup (500 mL) Pyrex measuring cup or beaker
- glass baking dish
- 2-quart (2-L) metal saucepan
- large glass or microwave-safe plastic bowl
- lab thermometer
- ½-gallon (2-L) pitcher of water
- timer or watch with second hand
- standard oven or large toaster oven
- stove or hot plate
- microwave oven
- oven mitt
- adult to assist you

Safety Note This experiment should be conducted under the guidance of a responsible adult. During this experiment, you will be using various devices to heat water, and the containers will be hot. Always use pot holders or oven mitts when handling the containers of water. Please review and follow the safety guidelines before proceeding.

Procedure

1. Before starting the experiment, fill the pitcher with ½ gallon (2 L) of water and allow it to stand on a counter or table for at least an hour so that the water reaches room temperature. Turn the oven to 500° F (260° C) and allow it to pre-heat for at least 10 minutes.

2. Use the measuring cup to pour 2 cups (500 mL) of water from the pitcher into the glass baking dish, the glass or plastic bowl, and the metal sauce-pan. Make certain that the amount of water in each container is exactly the same.

3. Place the thermometer in the water in the glass (plastic) bowl and allow it to stand for 30 seconds. Remove the thermometer and record the temperature of the water on the data table under the heading "Microwave/Starting Temperature." Place the bowl uncovered in the microwave. Set the microwave on high, and heat the bowl for one minute. Have an adult use the oven mitts or pot holders to remove the bowl from the microwave and carefully pour the hot water back into the measuring cup. Place the thermometer in the hot water for 30 seconds (see Figure 1) and record the temperature on the data table under the heading "Microwave/Ending Temperature." After recording the temperature, dispose of the water in the measuring cup.

4. Place the thermometer in the water in the metal saucepan, and allow it to stand for 30 seconds. Remove the thermometer and record the temperature of the water on the data table under the heading "Stove/Starting Temperature." Turn the burner of the stove on high and place the metal pan on the burner for one minute. If you are using an electric stove or hot plate, allow the heating element to warm up for 60 seconds before placing the pan on top of it. Have an adult use the pot holders to remove the saucepan from the stove and carefully pour the hot water into the empty measuring cup. Place the thermometer in the hot water for 30 seconds and record the temperature on the data table under the heading "Stove/Ending Temperature." After recording the temperature, dispose of the water in the measuring cup.

5. Place the thermometer in the water in the glass baking dish and allow it to stand for 30 seconds. Remove the thermometer and record the temperature of the water on the data table under the heading "Oven/Starting Temperature." After the oven has warmed up, place the baking dish on the center rack of the oven for 1 minute. After a minute has passed, have an adult use the oven mitts or pot holders to remove the baking dish from the oven and carefully pour the hot water into the empty measuring cup. Place the thermometer in the hot water for 30 seconds and record the temperature on the data table under the heading "Oven/Ending Temperature." After recording the temperature, dispose of the water in the measuring cup.

6. Calculate the change in temperature for each test by subtracting the starting temperature from the ending temperature and record the information on the data table.

Data Table 1			
	Ending Temperature	**Starting Temperature**	**Change in Temperature**
Microwave			
Stove			
Oven			

Analysis

1. Which way of heating the water showed the greatest temperature change in one minute?
2. What was the main form of heat transfer found in each of the three methods used for heating the water?
3. Why was it important to heat the water for the same amount of time and use the same amount of water in each container?
4. Why did you transfer the hot water to the measuring cup before taking its temperature?

 ## What's Going On?

The way we cook our food often determines how the food will look and taste. When you fry an egg in a metal pan, you use conduction to cook the egg. The heat travels through the metal pan to the egg. This type of heat transfer is rapid, and the egg cooks quickly. With conduction, the cooking isn't even. Because the heat must travel through the pan, the side of the food that is in contact with the surface of the pan gets cooked first. That's why when you fry something in a pan you usually have to flip it

When you bake bread or roast meat in an oven, the main form of heat transfer is convection. Convection is a slower process than conduction. Air inside the oven must first get heated by the flame or heating element. Then, hot air currents surround the food and the food cooks from the outside in. When food is cooked in an oven, the heat transfer is fairly even, so food does not have to be flipped or turned.

A microwave oven cooks food using radiation. A device called a magnetron creates electromagnetic waves. When these waves strike water or fat molecules in the food, the molecules begin to rapidly vibrate back and forth. The vibrations create friction, which heats the food, cooking it from the inside out. Because most foods have water or fat molecules in them, microwave radiation is an efficient way to cook. Unfortunately, if water molecules are not evenly distributed, a microwave can cook a food unevenly. In addition, because microwaves cook from the inside out, they don't brown the surface of foods. It gives some foods a rubbery texture. Because microwaves work primarily on water molecules, they are ideal for thawing frozen foods or reheating stews and other foods that have a great deal of moisture in them.

Our Findings

1. The stove should have given the greatest increase, followed by the microwave and then the oven.

2. The stove used conduction, the oven used convection, and the microwave used radiation.

3. In a controlled experiment, it is important to keep all the conditions the same.

4. Taking the temperature in the measuring cup eliminated the chance that the heated container would affect the temperature of the water.

POPPING CORN

Today we have hundreds of foods on which to snack, including chips, dips, and jerky strips. One snack food that has stood the test of time is popcorn. According to archaeologists, Native Americans first started enjoying this tasty treat around 7,000 years ago. It's still one of the more popular foods that people munch on today. Popcorn is a relative of sweet corn—the kind you eat on a cob. What makes it special is that the kernels have a tough, airtight outer layer called the hull. Inside the kernel is starch and a little water, which is the key. When popcorn kernels are heated, the liquid water inside begins to change into a gas, causing pressure to build. The vapor pressure finally reaches a critical stage; then, the kernel literally explodes, producing a fluffy white "blossom" that's delicious to eat.

When Native Americans first made popcorn, they did it over an open fire. Unfortunately, many of the kernels burned. Over the years, people have come up with better methods for popping corn. One way is to use a pan with a small amount of hot oil at the bottom. This method relies on conduction and still results in many burnt kernels. A hot-air popper uses convection. These are the kinds used in movie theaters. There are far fewer burnt kernels, but this method frequently leaves kernels

Corn is able to pop because, unlike most other grains, its kernels have a hard, moisture-sealed hull along with a dense, starchy filling. When heated, pressure builds inside the kernel, causing the corn to "explode."

unpopped. Without a doubt, the most effective way of making popcorn is in a microwave oven. Because the microwave radiation heats the water in the kernel from the inside out, the kernels pop, but the outer surface doesn't burn.

THE ADVANTAGES OF EATING COOKED FOOD

When it comes to eating, humans are unique among members of the animal kingdom. As far as scientists can tell, we are the only species that intentionally cooks its food. Other animals will eat food that has been cooked and processed, but we depend on cooking as a way of life. Cooking food offers several advantages over eating it raw. For one thing, cooked food often tastes better. Whether it's a baked potato, some roasted peppers, or a grilled hamburger, cooking food gives it a flavor that most people seem to enjoy. Cooking food also kills some of the bacteria that could make us sick. When it comes to vegetables, cooking produces one other big advantage. In **Experiment 12: Cooking Carrots**, you will discover what happens to vegetables when the heat is on!

EXPERIMENT 12

Cooking Carrots

Topic

What happens to vegetables when they are cooked?

Introduction

Before cooking food generally became the norm, people ate everything raw, as did other members of the animal kingdom. Evidence suggests that humans have been using fire for about 1.5 million years, but it is not clear if it was used for cooking, warmth, or defense from predators. By about 250,000 years ago, there is evidence that humans were cooking. Bits of charred animal bones found with the ashes of fire pits, along with burned seeds, suggest that some food was intentionally roasted. The first record of boiling food in water dates to around 12,700 years ago. At that time in Japan, clay pots were used to cook fish and vegetables. Today, boiling food in water is a common cooking technique.

In this activity, you will test to see what happens to carrots when they are boiled in water.

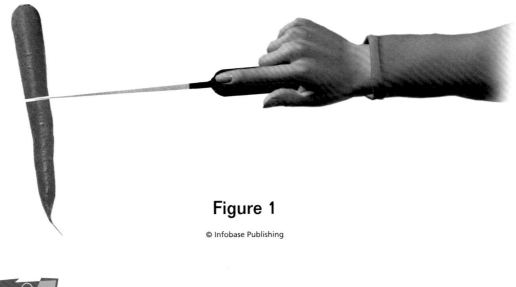

Figure 1

© Infobase Publishing

Time Required

60 minutes

Materials

- 2-quart (2-L) saucepan with lid

- 2-cup (500-mL) clear Pyrex beaker or measuring cup filled with cold water

- timer or watch with second hand

- stove or hot plate

- pot holder

- 6 peeled and cleaned baby carrots

- sharp kitchen knife

- cutting board

- plate

- slotted spoon

- adult to assist you

Safety Note This experiment should be conducted under the guidance of a responsible adult. During this experiment, you will be using a sharp knife and a stove to cut and cook carrots. Always use pot holders or oven mitts when handling the cooking utensils and pot. Please review and follow the safety guidelines before proceeding.

Procedure

1. Place one of the carrots on the cutting board. Cut the carrot in half across its long axis (Figure 1). Observe a piece of the carrot and taste it. Consider its texture (what it feels like), how easy it is to chew, and how it tastes. Record your observations on the data table.

2. Place the rest of the carrots into the pot. Observe the color of the water before pouring the water into the pot. Cover the carrots with the water. Place the lid on the pot and allow the carrots to stand undisturbed for 15 minutes. Remove the lid and observe the water. Use the slotted spoon to remove one of the carrots and repeat Step 1, making sure to record your observations on the data table.

3. Place the pot with the carrots on the stove or hot plate, and turn the burner or hot plate on high. Bring the water to a boil. Once the water starts boiling, reduce the heat and allow the carrots to simmer for 30 minutes. Turn off the heat and use the pot holder to remove the lid. Be careful not to burn yourself on the steam escaping from the pot. Use the slotted spoon to remove the rest of the carrots. Repeat Step 1 with one of the carrots. Allow it to cool for a few minutes before you taste it, so that you do not burn your mouth. Carefully pour the water from the pot into the beaker or measuring cup and observe it for any changes. Record your observations on the data table.

Data Table 1	
Description of raw carrot	
Description of carrot after soaking in cold water for 15 minutes	
Description of carrot after cooking for 30 minutes	

Analysis

1. What happened to a carrot after it soaked in cold water for 15 minutes?
2. What happened to a carrot after it was cooked for 30 minutes?
3. What happened to the water after the carrots were cooked in it?
4. What did you smell when you removed the lid after the carrots finished cooking?

What's Going On?

There are several reasons that people cook food. Cooking often makes food more digestible and easier to chew. Cooking also enhances the flavors of some foods. When most foods are heated, they undergo chemical changes. Vegetables—such as carrots, potatoes, and yams—become softer and are easier to digest. While carrots can be eaten raw, potatoes and yams can't be fully digested by humans unless the vegetables are cooked. As a carrot is heated, some of the hemi-cellulose fibers break down. These fibers give a carrot its shape, so when they break down the carrot gets softer. The breakdown also makes the carrot easier to digest and more nutritious. A carrot often will taste sweeter after cooking because some of the sugars have been released and concentrated.

Even after cooking, carrots retain most of their color. The orange color found in carrots comes from a pigment called carotene. Green vegetables, such as broccoli, get their color from a pigment called chlorophyll. Carotenes do not dissolve in water and are not affected by normal cooking temperatures. As a result the water that the carrots were cooked in turned only slightly orange. However, when broccoli is cooked in water for a long time, the green color fades, because the water removes the chlorophyll from the food.

Our Findings

1. There was no apparent change in the carrots or the water after the carrots soaked in the cold water for 15 minutes.

2. After the carrots cooked in the water, they were much softer and easier to cut and chew. The carrot was slightly paler, and it might have tasted sweeter.

3. After the carrots cooked in the water, the water had a slight orange color.

4. When the lid was removed, there was a sweet smell coming from the pot.

THE EFFECT OF TEMPERATURE ON FOOD

As we saw in the previous experiment, cooking involves heat. When food is heated, a chemical change usually takes place. In some cases, the changes can be dramatic and fast. Take toast, for instance. If you have ever left a slice of bread in a toaster a bit too long, you know that it goes fairly quickly from golden brown to burned. In other cases, the change is slow and steady. Roasting a turkey in a conventional oven can take hours, but the results are well worth it. One of the main factors controlling the rate of these changes is the temperature of the oven, water, or pan in which the cooking is being done. In **Experiment 13: Heating Water for Tea**, you will test to see the effect of water temperature on the solubility of the substances found in tea leaves as you brew a cup of tea.

Steeping is the process of allowing a tea bag to sit in water in order for it to extract color and flavor into the water.

EXPERIMENT 13

Heating Water for Tea

Topic

How does the temperature of the water affect the solubility of the chemical substances found in tea?

Introduction

Tea is a popular beverage; people drink it in just about every country in the world. Most common types of tea (including black tea, white tea, green tea, and oolong tea) are made from the leaves and buds of the tea plant *Camellia sinensis,* which is native throughout Southeast Asia. Today, tea plants are cultivated on plantations in warmer climates all over the world. Historians aren't sure when people started brewing tea, but records show that it was being made in ancient China more than 2,000 years ago. The standard way of brewing tea is to take the leaves and steep them in water for several minutes. The water removes different chemical compounds from the leaves, which give tea its taste. In this experiment, you are going to test to see if changing the temperature of the water has any effect on the rate of the chemical reactions.

Time Required

60 minutes for preparation, 30 minutes for the experiment

Materials

- 3 large (12-oz) disposable cups for hot beverages
- 3 large (12-oz) disposable clear plastic drinking glasses
- 3 identical bags of black tea
- marker
- sheet of plain white copier paper
- Pyrex measuring cup or graduated cylinder
- tea kettle or pot for boiling water

- refrigerator or cooler filled with ice

- 2 bottles, each filled with about 2 cups (½ L) of water

- timer or watch with second hand

- oven mitt or pot holder

- adult to assist you

Safety Note This experiment should be conducted under the guidance of a responsible adult. Use pot holders or oven mitts when handling the tea kettle. Please review and follow the safety guidelines before proceeding.

Procedure

1. One hour before starting the experiment, place one bottle of water in a refrigerator or cooler packed with ice. Place the second bottle of water on a counter, until it reaches room temperature. Five minutes before starting the experiment, fill a tea kettle or saucepan with 2 cups (½ L) of water and begin heating it on a stove or hot plate so that it comes to a boil.

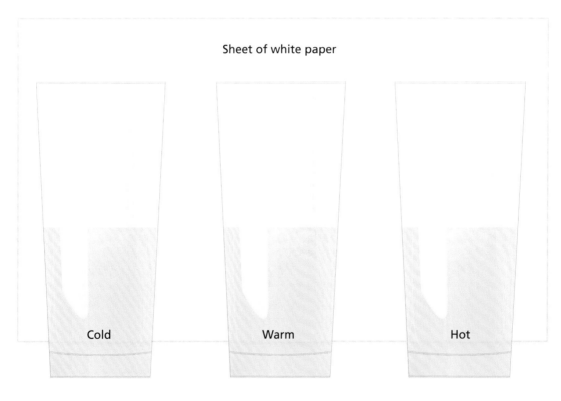

Sheet of white paper

Cold   Warm   Hot

Figure 1

2. Label the three hot-beverage cups "cold," "warm," and "hot." Do the same for the three plastic drinking glasses. Place a tea bag in each of the hot-beverage cups. Make certain that the label with the top of the string stays on the outside of the cup.

3. Pour 1 cup (250 mL) of the cold water into the cup labeled "cold." Allow the tea bag to soak undisturbed in the water for three minutes. Remove the bag.

4. Pour 250 mL (1 cup) from the bottle of water on the counter into the cup labeled "warm." Allow the tea bag to soak undisturbed in the water for three minutes. Remove the bag.

5. Once the water in the tea kettle or saucepan starts boiling, turn off the heat and allow it to stand for about 30 seconds. Use the measuring cup to pour 1 cup (250 mL) of hot water into the cup labeled "hot." Use the pot holder when pouring the hot water. Allow the tea bag to soak undisturbed in the water for three minutes. Remove the bag.

6. Pour the tea made with the cold water into the clear cup labeled "cold." Do the same for the other two cups of tea. Place the three glasses side by side on a counter and hold the sheet of white paper behind them so that it acts like a screen (see Figure 1). Compare the color of the tea in each of the glasses. Smell the tea in each of the three glasses and compare the odors. Take a small sip of each cup and compare the tastes. Record your observations on the data table.

Data Table 1			
	Color	**Odor**	**Taste**
Cold tea			
Warm tea			
Hot tea			

Analysis

1. Which cup of tea had the darkest color?
2. Which cup of tea had the strongest odor?
3. Which cup of tea had the strongest taste?
4. Based on your data, what is the best water temperature for brewing black tea?

What's Going On?

Black tea, like coffee, brews the fastest when the water used is just below its normal boiling point of 212°F (100°C). This is explained by the kinetic-molecular theory. The molecules that make up matter are in constant motion. As temperature increases, so does the rate of molecular motion. When a chemical reaction takes place, increasing the molecular motion increases the chances of molecules colliding and interacting with each other. More heat in a reaction also increases the energy available to break chemical bonds, which means molecules can then form new substances.

When tea is brewed, the water reacts with alkaloid salts found in the leaves of the tea plant to produce substances known as tannins. Tannins give tea its color and slightly bitter flavor. Some teas also contain caffeine, which is bitter. These days, the term *tea* is also used to describe many beverages that are not made from the leaves of tea plants. Often herbal teas are made from other plants. Even with traditional tea, there are a number of varieties based on the way the tea leaves are processed. Black tea, green tea, and white tea all come from the leaves of the same plant, but they are processed differently. The flavors of each of these teas are enhanced by brewing them at various temperatures for different periods of time. Black tea should be brewed for about three minutes, using water that is close to the boiling point at 212°F or 100°C. Green tea is also usually brewed for about three minutes, but the water temperature is lower, about 170°F (77°C). White tea, which has the most delicate flavor, should be brewed for about two minutes with water that is about 150°F (66°C).

Our Findings

1. The tea made with the hot water had the darkest color.
2. The tea made with the hot water had the strongest odor.
3. The tea made with the hot water had the strongest taste.
4. The best way to make black tea is with water that has just reached the boiling point.

MELTING AND FREEZING MATTER

Temperature can cause matter to change its state. That doesn't mean it moves from New York to South Dakota; it means changing from solid, liquid, or gas to another physical state. At different temperatures, matter will change from one state to another. Pure water will turn from liquid to gas when it is heated to 212°F (100°C). It will turn solid, or freeze, at 32°F (0°C). As it turns out, solid water (also known as ice) will melt at the same temperature. Melting and freezing are examples of physical changes; they can be reversed. They also are important processes in cooking. Sometimes a physical change can also be accompanied by a chemical change. In **Experiment 14:** *Melting Sugar,* you will melt some matter and determine if the change is purely physical or not. In the process, you will make a sweet treat.

Ice cubes are usually preferred over crushed ice in many drinks because they take longer to melt and, therefore, keep drinks cool for a longer period of time.

Melting Sugar

Topic

Is the melting of sugar an example of a physical change or a chemical change?

Introduction

Melting and freezing are physical changes. A physical change is reversible. A piece of ice can be melted and refrozen by heating it and cooling it again. The water has changed its state, but it is still water. During a chemical change, molecules will rearrange and new chemical compounds will form. Chemical changes cannot be reversed. In this experiment, you will test to see if the melting of sugar is a physical change or a chemical change.

Time Required

45 minutes

Materials

- ¼ cup (100 mL) white cane sugar
- small saucepan or frying pan
- wooden spoon
- small sheet of aluminum foil
- clean tongue depressor
- stove or hot plate
- 2 oven mitts
- adult to assist you

Procedure

1. Pour the sugar into the bottom of a dry saucepan and place it on a stove or hot plate. Turn the heat to medium. Stir the sugar every 30 seconds with the wooden spoon to keep it from burning. After a few minutes, the sugar will begin to melt.

2. Continue stirring the sugar until all of it has melted. Turn off the heat. Smell the sugar in the pot by wafting some of the air toward your nose (see Figure 1).

3. After the sugar has cooled for about one minute, twirl the end of the tongue depressor in the sugar so that some of the sugar sticks to it. Be careful

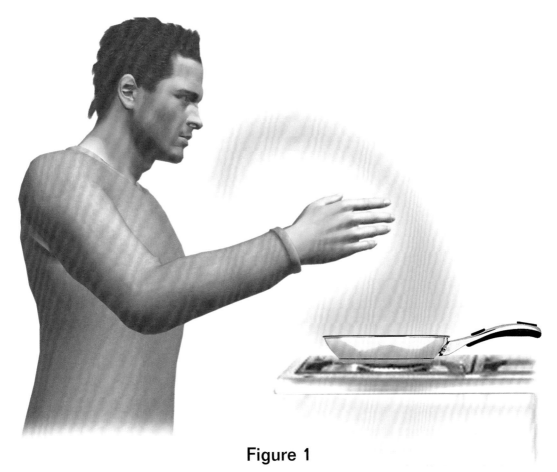

Figure 1

because the sugar will be hot. Lift the tongue depressor out of the sugar and hold it over the pan, so that any drops fall back into the pan. Lay the tongue depressor on a piece of aluminum foil and allow it to cool for 10 minutes.

4. After the sugar on the tongue depressor has completed cooled, lick the sugar on the top of the tongue depressor. Compare the taste to the taste of some fresh sugar crystals. After you have finished, fill the saucepan with water and allow it and the wooden spoon to soak for about 10 minutes. The sugar should dissolve. Then, wash them both with regular soap and water.

Analysis

1. What color did the sugar turn as it began to melt?
2. How did the melted sugar smell?
3. How did the taste of the sugar on the tongue depressor compare with the taste of the fresh sugar crystals?
4. Based on your observations, was this a physical change or a chemical change?

 ## What's Going On?

Like most substances, cane sugar will melt if the temperature gets hot enough. Unlike ice, which melts at 32°F (0°C), table sugar melts at a much higher temperature, usually around 320°F (160°C). When the sugar begins to change to a liquid, it also undergoes a chemical reaction called caramelization. As the sugar is heated, some of the water molecules in the sugar crystals begin to evaporate. This changes the chemical structure of the sugar. When the sugar finally melts, more water is driven off, setting off a chain of reactions. At about 338°F (168°C), the liquid sugar starts to change color. It turns amber, and then a deep golden brown. At this point, it has changed from plain sugar to caramel. Not only has the color changed, but also the taste. Instead of being only sweet, it also has a slightly nutty roasted flavor that's delicious on candy apples and ice cream. The caramel that results from melting sugar is not the same as the soft caramels sold in a candy store. Those caramel candies are made from sugar, cream, corn syrup, and butter.

Our Findings

1. As it melted, the sugar began to turn an amber color.
2. The melted sugar smelled a little like toasted marshmallows.
3. The sugar on the tongue depressor was not as sweet as the sugar crystals.
4. The melting of the sugar was both a physical and chemical change.

CHILLING OUT

When it comes to preparing food, adding heat is only half the story. Sometimes you want to remove heat to cool something. Beverages such as lemonade, milk, and water tend to taste better when they are cold, as do foods like gelatin and pudding. In the same way that melting brings about changes in foods, so does freezing. In **Experiment 15: *How Freezing Food Affects Quality*,** you will test the effects of freezing on a variety of different food items to see which ones best stand up to the cold.

Freezing prepackaged meals tends to lessen their flavor, so manufacturers usually add more salt and fat to improve the taste for consumers.

How Freezing Food Affects Quality

Topic

How does freezing affect the quality of food?

Introduction

One of the best ways to preserve food is by freezing it. When foods are frozen, the growth of bacteria and fungi—which normally cause food to spoil—is slowed tremendously. The ability to freeze certain foods also has made life more convenient. Instead of preparing a meal from scratch, people can now buy pre-packaged frozen dinners and snacks, which they have only to heat and eat. If you take a trip down the frozen foods aisle of a grocery store, you'll find that many foods, such as pizza, pasta, corn, and carrots, come frozen and ready to eat. When foods are frozen and then thawed, do they undergo any changes? In this activity you will freeze a variety of foods to see how they stack up to their fresh counterparts when it comes to texture and taste.

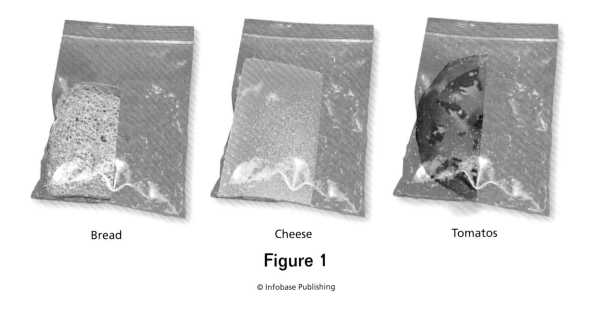

Bread   Cheese   Tomatos

Figure 1

© Infobase Publishing

Time Required

20 minutes for preparation, 1 day for freezing, and 20 minutes for observations

Materials

- 12 zipper-style sandwich bags

- fresh tomato

- slice of processed American cheese

- small chunk of aged cheddar cheese

- slice of bologna

- small stick of pepperoni or similar cooked dried sausage

- slice of white or wheat bread

- kitchen knife

- cutting board

- small plastic bottle with cap

- water

- freezer

- refrigerator

- sink

- paper towels

- adult to assist you

Safety Note This experiment should be conducted under the guidance of a responsible adult. Use caution when using the knife to cut the food samples. Please review and follow the safety guidelines before proceeding.

Procedure

1. Before starting the experiment, wash your hands thoroughly with soap and hot water. Also wash the tomato and pat it try with a paper towel. On a clean cutting board, cut each of the food samples in half. Rinse and dry the knife after you cut each sample. Place one half of each sample in one plastic bag and put the other half inside another plastic bag. Make sure each sample is in a separate bag. Before sealing each bag, try to get as much air out of it as possible. Place one set of sealed bags in the freezer

and the other set in the refrigerator. Allow them to rest undisturbed, for 24 hours.

2. Fill the plastic bottle to the very top with water and screw the cap on tightly. Place the bottle of water in the freezer next to the food samples and allow it to stand for 24 hours.

3. After 24 hours have passed, remove the food samples from the freezer and refrigerator and place them on a table or counter. Allow the frozen samples to thaw for about ½ hour. Remove the water bottle from the freezer and examine it closely. Record your observations of the bottle on the data table.

4. Remove each of the refrigerated samples of food from its bag and place them on a paper towel. Examine each sample closely. Try breaking or tearing the sample with your fingers to test its texture and, if you want, taste each sample to check its flavor. Record your observations of the fresh food samples and then discard any leftover samples, along with the paper towels.

5. After the frozen samples have thawed, remove each one from its bag and place it on a paper towel. Repeat the procedure from Step 4 and record your observations on the data table.

Data Table 1	
Observations of Refrigerated Food Samples	
Tomato	
American cheese	
Cheddar cheese	
Bologna	
Pepperoni	
Bread	

Data Table 2	
Observations of Frozen Water Bottle	

Data Table 3	
Observations of Frozen Food Samples After They Thawed	
Tomato	
American cheese	
Cheddar cheese	
Bologna	
Pepperoni	
Bread	

Analysis

1. How did the bottle of water appear when you removed it from the freezer?
2. How did the texture of the frozen food samples compare with the refrigerated food samples?
3. Which samples showed the greatest difference after thawing?
4. Which samples showed the least amount of change after thawing?
5. Based on your data, what is the controlling factor on how well a food reacts to freezing and thawing?

What's Going On?

When foods are frozen, the water in them turns to ice. When most substances change from a liquid state to a solid state, they contract. The volume decreases and they become denser. Water does the exact opposite. When water turns to ice, it expands and becomes less dense. This is why ice cubes float on top of a glass of water. Typically, water expands 9% when it changes from a liquid to a solid. This is why the bottle of water burst when it was frozen. The same thing happens to the water contained in the cells of food. As the water expands, it breaks the cell walls. When the food thaws, it is limp and soggy and has lost much of its crispness. Because fruits and vegetables have a higher water content then meat, they tend to be affected more than meat products. Because the pepperoni is dried, it has a very low water content, so freezing had little effect on it.

Before the early 1900s, frozen food as we know it today did not really exist. Refrigerators and freezers were still quite rare. As technology improved, more people tried freezing foods as a means of preserving them and discovered the problem of the destruction of cell walls. In the early 1920s, people began experimenting with ways of "flash freezing" foods. The idea behind this technique is to freeze foods so quickly that ice crystals would not have a chance to grow. In 1924, inventor Clarence Birdseye developed two methods for quick-freezing. His inventions revolutionized the food industry; he is often considered to be the "father of frozen food." Although he died in 1956, Birds Eye Foods is still a major leader in the frozen food industry.

Our Findings

1. The water in the bottle expanded and burst the bottle.
2. With the exception of the pepperoni, the food samples seemed less crisp and a bit soggier than when they were fresh.
3. The tomato, American cheese, and bread changed the most.
4. The pepperoni changed the least.
5. The main factor controlling the effects of freezing on foods is water content.

FREEZER BURN AND CRUNCHY ICE CREAM

Have you ever eaten some ice cream that has been sitting in an open container in the back of the freezer for a few weeks? It just doesn't taste right. The biggest change is that the ice cream is crunchy—and not because it's supposed to be. When foods are kept for a long time in a freezer, some of the water molecules evaporate by a process known as **sublimation**. They go from a solid directly to a gas. When this happens to ice cream, it causes it to become denser. Ice crystals start to develop, ruining the smooth, creamy texture.

Sublimation also happens to meat and fish that have not been properly stored in the freezer. If you have ever looked at a piece of frozen meat that has been wrapped loosely in foil or plastic, you have probably noticed that the surface is discolored with white spots. It almost looks as if it has been cooked. What you are seeing is called freezer burn.

Water molecules escape from the surface of the food, resulting in a dried-out piece of meat. Double-wrapping the food and placing it in an air-tight container can minimize freezer burn. Even this method can only protect the food for so long. The best thing to do is to regularly check the foods in the freezer and use them before sublimation causes you to lose them.

SCREAM FOR ICE CREAM

One of the most popular frozen foods is ice cream. These days, ice cream companies make up one of the fastest growing sectors of the food industry. Modern technology has allowed manufacturers to produce an incredible array of ice cream and frozen desserts, but ice cream wasn't always easy to come by. Before the development of electric freezers, people had to work very hard to make their own ice cream. In **Experiment 16:** *Lowering the Freezing Point of Water*, you will have the opportunity to make your own delicious frozen dessert using some ice and elbow grease.

Lowering the Freezing Point of Water

Topic

How can the freezing point of water be lowered?

Introduction

Long before there were commercial freezers, people were enjoying frozen confections such as ice cream, frozen custard, and sherbet. According to historians, Marco Polo uncovered the secret for making ice cream in his travels to the Far East and brought it back to Europe more than 700 years ago. The first commercial ice cream establishment was set up in Paris in 1670, more than 150 years before the modern freezer was invented. In this activity, you will discover how a simple combination of chemicals and some muscle power can have chilling results.

Crushed ice

Container of milk mixture

Cutaway view showing interior of coffee can

Figure 1

Time Required

45 minutes

Materials

- empty coffee can with lid
- small plastic container with tight-fitting lid to fit inside coffee can
- lab thermometer
- milk
- chocolate or strawberry syrup
- large drinking glass
- measuring cup
- 2 teaspoons
- hammer
- dish towel
- large bowl
- large container of salt
- 20 to 30 ice cubes
- freezer
- timer or watch
- gloves
- friend to assist you

Safety Note Use gloves when shaking the coffee can. Please review and follow the safety guidelines before proceeding.

Procedure

1. Use the spoon and syrup to mix a glass of chocolate or strawberry milk. Pour some of the milk into the small plastic container and snap the lid on tight. Place a few ice cubes inside the dish towel and use the hammer to crush them into smaller pieces. Continue crushing ice until you have filled most of the bowl with crushed ice.

2. Fill the bottom of the coffee can with crushed ice and put the plastic container inside, on top of the ice. Fill the rest of the can with crushed ice. Pack the ice chips around the sides of the plastic container. Snap the lid on the coffee can. Place the bowl with the crushed ice back in the freezer so that you have ice to use for the second part of the experiment.

3. Put on the gloves and begin shaking the can vigorously for 10 minutes. If you have a friend with you, take turns shaking the can so that you don't get tired. After 10 minutes, remove the lid. Place the thermometer inside the can so that it is resting in the ice water and allow it to stand for one minute. Read and record the temperature of the ice. Remove the plastic container from the coffee can and open the lid. Observe the milk mixture.

4. Close the lid on the plastic container and place it back in the coffee can. Repack the can with crushed ice in the same manner as you did in Step 2. Before closing the lid, add 1 cup (250 mL) of salt to the ice inside the can. Snap the lid back on the coffee can and repeat Step 3. After you have observed the milk mixture a second time, enjoy the results of your labor!

Analysis

1. What happened to the milk mixture after shaking the can the first time?
2. What was the temperature of the ice water inside the can after the first trial?
3. What happened to the milk mixture after shaking the can with the salt mixed in the ice?
4. What was the temperature of the salt water inside the can after the second trial?

 ### What's Going On?

Before gas or electric freezers, people made ice cream and other frozen confections using a mechanical freezer. These devices had an inner chamber for the mixture that was to be frozen and an outer chamber filled with ice and salt. Turning a crank would mix the contents in the inner chamber. After a few minutes, the mixture would freeze. When salt is mixed with ice, it lowers the temperature of the ice several degrees below its normal melting point. This is why salt is spread on icy roads. It causes the ice to melt, even when the air temperature is below the freezing point of water.

When you did the first trial, you used plain ice in the coffee can. No matter how much you shook the can, the temperature inside the can never got below the freezing point of the milk mixture in the inner container. That's because milk freezes at about the same temperature as water. The milk may have gotten really cold, but it could not freeze because the temperature of the ice water surrounding it was not below 32°F (0°C). Once the salt was added to the ice, the temperature in the coffee can dropped below the freezing point of the milk and it began to turn solid. Shaking the can kept the mixture agitated so that it was able to freeze evenly.

Our Findings

1. There was no change in the milk mixture other than getting colder.
2. The temperature of the ice water should have been 32°F (0°C) or slightly above.
3. The milk mixture should have started to freeze.
4. The temperature of the salt water should have been lower than 32°F (0°C).

ASTRONAUT ICE CREAM AND FREEZE-DRIED FOODS

Before we conclude this section on heating and cooling, we must look at one other special way that people have discovered to preserve food. The method is called lyophilization, but its common name is freeze-drying. As the name suggests, it involves both freezing and evaporating water from food. The freeze-drying of food was first developed by scientists at the National Aeronautic and Space Administration (NASA) in the 1960s. They were looking for a way to preserve food and reduce its weight. The trick is to remove the water without destroying the structure and texture of the food. When it's time to eat, just add water, and presto—the food is back in its original form!

Freeze drying depends on the process of sublimation—the process of turning solid ice directly to a gas. You may recall that sublimation is also responsible for freezer burn. When foods are freeze dried, sublimation occurs very quickly. After the foods are frozen, they are placed in a vacuum chamber, where most of the air is sucked out. Then heating elements are turned

Early freeze-dried astronaut food was often a bit bland. In 2006, chef Emeril Lagasse of the Food Network created packaged meals for astronauts to eat in space. Some astronauts serving for long periods in space at the International Space Station noted that their perception of taste decreases a bit in space, so they longed for spicier, more flavorful foods, such as Lagasse's jambalaya, garlic green beans, and mashed potatoes with bacon.

on, which causes the ice in the food to change directly to a gas. What's left is perfectly preserved dehydrated food.

Even though freeze-dried foods were first developed for the space program, they have found a great many uses right here on Earth. The armed forces often use freeze-dried foods on patrol, and so do hikers and campers who want to reduce the loads they are carrying. Many forms of instant coffee are freeze-dried. One tasty freeze-dried food is astronaut ice cream. Packed in a foil pouch, it looks and tastes like the real thing but it is not cold. Because it is dried, it sort of tingles on your tongue when you eat it. We will begin the next chapter with a look at the tongue as we explore what controls the taste and smell of some foods.

Sugar and Spice

Have you ever had an experience in which a food looked delicious, but as soon as you tasted it, you changed your mind? Maybe it was a cake that was just too sweet, or a sauce that had too much onion or garlic in it. No matter how appetizing a food looks, it also has to taste good. Taste—along with touch, sight, smell, and hearing—make up the five main senses that we depend on to get us through our lives. Our senses are designed to provide us with information about the world around us. Though they may seem to work separately, they often work together.

As you might have guessed, the human sense of taste is concentrated in the mouth. Specialized groups of cells called taste buds are found all over the mouth but are concentrated mostly on the tongue. A typical tongue may have as many as 9,000 taste buds. Each one consists of a cluster of receptor cells, which detect chemicals in food. The cells then send a signal to the brain for evaluation. Based on the signals, the brain decides whether the food should be swallowed or spit out. Taste buds protect us from eating foods that may be rotten or poisonous. The tongue is the primary organ of taste, but it does not work alone. In **Experiment 17: *Smell and Taste*,** you will discover how these two senses work together to allow you to enjoy the flavor of your favorite foods.

EXPERIMENT 17

Smell and Taste

Topic

How are the senses of taste and smell related?

Introduction

Humans have five basic taste sensations: sweet, sour, bitter, salty, and something called umami, which is a savory sort of flavor that does not fit into any of the other categories. As it turns out, a single receptor cell can detect only one of these. Taste buds on the tip of the tongue are more sensitive to sweet and salty flavors. Those on the side of the tongue are more sensitive to sour flavors. The taste buds for bitter are the most sensitive, and they are concentrated at the base of the tongue. Because many of the substances that are potentially poisonous tend to be bitter, these taste buds serve as a final warning system to prevent us from swallowing them. Taste buds get a lot of use. They last only a few days before your body replaces them. However, your taste buds don't work alone. In this activity, you will discover that your brain also relies on your nose to determine the true flavor of certain foods.

Time Required

30 minutes prep time and an additional 30 minutes for the experiment

Materials

- knife
- ruler
- cutting board
- toothpicks
- roll of paper towels or aluminum foil
- paper plates

- blindfold

- glass of water for each test subject

- raw potatoes

- apples

- pears

- cucumbers

- cantaloupes

- 2 or 3 people to serve as test subjects

Safety Note Before conducting this experiment, check with each test subject to make certain that they do not have any allergies to any of the foods that you are using in the experiment. Please review and follow the safety guidelines before proceeding.

Procedure

1. Before conducting the experiment, cut the food samples into ½-in. (1-cm) cubes. Try to eliminate all seeds and peels. Prepare two cubes of each sample for each person. Place a toothpick in each cube (see Figure 1.) Cover each plate with a piece of foil or a paper towel so that the subjects cannot see the food samples.

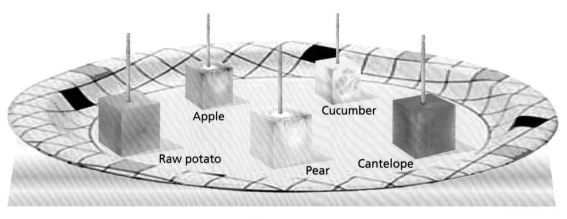

Figure 1

2. Before conducting the taste test ask the test subjects if they have any food allergies. If any do, they should not participate in the experiment. Tell the subjects that they will taste a number of fruits and vegetables, but do not let them know what the food samples will be. Blindfold the people or have them close their eyes. Ask them to pinch their noses closed. Have them each take one cube off the first plate and taste it. Ask each person to identify the food being sampled. Do not tell them if they are correct. Record the answers on the data table under the heading "Trial 1." Place a "Y" in the box if the person answered correctly and an "N" if he or she was incorrect. Have each person take a sip of water after tasting each sample. Repeat this procedure, one cube at a time, until all the foods have been sampled.

3. After you have completed the first trial, repeat the trial, following the same procedure used in Step 2. This time, allow people to sample the foods without holding their noses closed. Serve the food samples in a different order than you did during the first trial. Record the results on the data table under the heading "Trial 2." Compare the results of the trials.

Data Table 1										
Subject Name	**Potato**		**Apple**		**Cucumber**		**Cantaloupe**		**Pear**	
	Trial #1	Trial #2	Trial #1	Trial #2	Trial #1	Trial #2	Trial #1	Trial #2	Trial #1	Trial #2

Analysis

1. Were some foods easier to identify than others?
2. Do your results indicate that the sense of taste depends on the sense of smell?
3. Did each person have the same results?
4. Some people lose their sense of taste when they have a cold. Do your results explain why this may happen?

 ## What's Going On?

Our taste buds do not work alone. Our sense of smell also plays a big role in allowing us to determine the taste of foods. This is particularly true of bland foods, which were used in this test. Your sense of smell is based in your nose. It relies on specialized cells known as olfactory receptors. There are as many as 20 million olfactory receptors in the human nose that allow us to distinguish more than 10,000 scents. When you eat food, the scent usually reaches your brain before the taste does. This allows you to determine if a food is rotten before you eat it. It is the combination of the scent of the food and the taste that produces the flavor. When your nose is blocked, or when you have a cold, you lose some ability to taste.

Our Findings

1. Foods with stronger flavors (cantaloupe) are usually easier to identify than bland foods (raw potato).
2. Subjects should have had more accurate results when they were allowed to smell the food while tasting it.
3. Even though the foods were the same, each person may have had different results because each person's sensitivity to taste and smell is different.
4. When you have a cold, you can't smell food as well, which interferes with your ability to taste.

SOME LIKE IT HOT

When it comes to eating different foods, tastes and tolerances vary. Some people enjoy the taste of onion and garlic, for example, while others find these flavors difficult to swallow. One of the most interesting differences in taste involves hot (spicy) foods. Certain foods are naturally spicy. Some forms of mustard and horseradish can be spicy, but for some real heat, check out chili peppers. Chili peppers are anything but chilly! The heat of a pepper is measured in something called Scoville Heat Units, or SHU for short. In 1912, chemist Wilbur Scoville devised the process for measuring heat intensity in peppers. Peppers get their kick from a chemical called capsaicin. The greater the concentration of capsaicin, the hotter the pepper, and the higher its ranking in Scoville Heat Units (SHU).

A common green bell pepper has almost no heat; it comes in at around 100 SHU. A New Mexico green chili is hot, but most people can tolerate it. It rates about a 1,500 on the Scoville scale. A typical jalapeno—which many people enjoy on nachos—falls between 3,000 and 6,000 SHU. A red chili pepper can reach 50,000 SHU. If you really want to play with fire, you have to try the Red Savina Habanero. It is the highest-ranking chili pepper on the Scoville scale, coming in at 300,000 SHU. So which pepper is the hottest in the world? That would be the Naga Jolokia from India, which has been measured at more than 1 million SHU!

FLAVOR EXTRACTS

Some people can eat raw chili peppers with no ill effects, but more often than not, people like to control the levels of spice in their foods. One way this is done is by using flavor extracts. Tabasco sauce, for example, is made by extracting some of the flavor and heat from fermented, ground Tabasco peppers. If you want just a hint of heat, you can use a few drops, but if you really want to spice things up, you can pour in most of a bottle. Peppers aren't the only plants from which people extract flavors. In **Experiment 18:** *Extracting Flavors from Foods,* you will try your hand at making your own natural flavor extracts from two common plants.

Extracting Flavors from Foods

Topic

How are natural flavors extracted from foods?

Introduction

Many of the foods and drinks that we consume every day are flavored with natural chemicals that have been extracted from parts of plants. Some of the most common extracts are taken from the juices of fruits, including oranges, lemons, apples, and raspberries. Coffee, vanilla, and chocolate all come from the beans of plants. People also have learned how to extract flavor from plant roots and even tree bark. In most cases, before flavors can be extracted from plants, the plant parts have to be processed in some way. In this activity, you will use two methods to extract cinnamon and ginger from their natural plant parts and test to see how these flavors can be concentrated in a liquid solution.

Time Required

90 minutes

Materials

- ¼-cup (125-mL) measuring cup
- ½-cup (250-mL) measuring cup
- 1-cup (500-mL) measuring cup or beaker
- 12 paper cups meant to hold hot liquids
- marker
- roll of aluminum foil
- watch or timer
- small piece of fresh ginger (available at most grocery stores)
- container of cinnamon sticks (available in spice aisle of grocery stores)
- sharp kitchen knife

- soup ladle

- cutting board

- small saucepan with cover

- tea kettle

- glass of water

- teaspoon

- stove or hot plate

- sink

- adult to assist you

Safety Note This experiment should be conducted under the guidance of a responsible adult. During this experiment you will be boiling water and using a sharp knife to cut different plant parts. Please review and follow the safety guidelines before proceeding.

Procedure

1. Before starting the experiment, use the marker to label the 12 cups as follows: "Boiled Ginger 5 Minutes," "Boiled Ginger 10 Minutes," "Boiled Ginger 15 Minutes," "Boiled Cinnamon 5 Minutes," "Boiled Cinnamon 10 Minutes," "Boiled Cinnamon 15 Minutes," "Steeped Ginger 5 Minutes," "Steeped Ginger 10 Minutes," "Steeped Ginger 15 Minutes," "Steeped Cinnamon 5 Minutes," "Steeped Cinnamon 10 Minutes," and "Steeped Cinnamon 15 Minutes." Place the cups on a counter or table in the grid pattern shown in Figure 1.

2. Fill the saucepan with 1 cup (500 mL) of water and place it on a stove or hot plate to boil. Smell the fresh ginger. Have an adult use the knife to cut the ginger into ½-in (1-cm) cubes. Fill the ½-cup measuring cup with the cut pieces of ginger and then smell them. Compare the scent of the cut ginger to the uncut ginger.

3. Once the water in the saucepan begins to boil, add ¼ cup of cut ginger. Keep the rest of the cut ginger off to the side. Place the lid on the saucepan and turn down the heat so that the ginger is simmering. Allow the ginger to simmer for five minutes. Remove about ¼ cup of water from the saucepan and place it in the cup marked "Boiled Ginger 5 Minutes." Cover the cup with a small piece of foil. Replace the saucepan lid and allow the ginger to

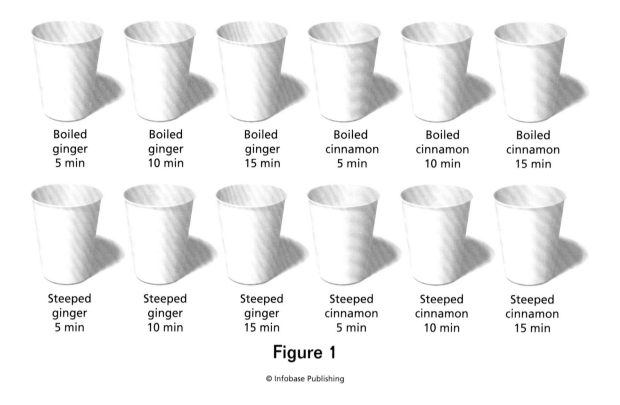

Figure 1

© Infobase Publishing

simmer for 5 more minutes. Repeat the same procedure after the ginger has boiled for 10 minutes and 15 minutes, making certain to put the ginger water in the correct cups. After you have filled the third cup with ginger water, dispose of the cooked ginger root and rinse the saucepan.

4. Fill the saucepan with 1 cup (500 mL) of water and place it on a stove or hot plate to boil. Break a stick of cinnamon in half. Once the water in the pan comes to a boil, place both halves of the broken cinnamon stick in the water and cover the pan. Follow the same procedure that you did with the ginger in Step 3.

5. Fill a tea kettle with water and place it on the stove or hot plate until it comes to a boil. Place the remaining ¼ cup of cut ginger into a 1-cup (500-mL) measuring cup. When the water boils, fill this measuring cup with boiling water. Allow the ginger to soak in the hot water for 5 minutes. Pour ¼ cup (125 mL) of water from the measuring cup into the cup labeled "Steeped Ginger 5 Minutes." Cover the cup with foil. Repeat the procedure after the ginger has steeped for 10 minutes and then 15 minutes, making certain to put the ginger water in the correct cups. After you have filled the third cup with ginger water, dispose of the steeped ginger root and rinse the measuring cup.

6. Repeat the procedure in Step 5 with a fresh stick of cinnamon that has been broken in half.

7. Remove the foil covers and compare the color and scent of each flavor extract. Record your observations. Use a teaspoon to taste each sample.

After each taste, rinse the spoon with clean water and take a sip of water to rinse your mouth. Compare the flavors in each cup and record your observations. Use your observations to answer the questions in the analysis section.

Analysis

1. What happened to the color, scent, and taste of the extracts as you boiled the ginger and cinnamon for longer periods of time?
2. What happened to the color, scent, and taste of the extracts as you steeped the ginger and cinnamon for longer periods of time?
3. Did boiling or steeping produce stronger flavors?

 ## What's Going On?

Cinnamon comes from the inner bark of several different tree species that grow in Asia. They all belong to the genus *Cinnamomum*. Most often the bark is dried, ground, and used as a powder. The flavor also can be extracted by placing the bark in hot water and allowing it to soak or steep for several minutes. This is the same way that flavor is extracted from tea leaves. The longer the bark soaks in the water, the more concentrated the flavor becomes. Steeping produces a slightly sweet aroma and delicate flavor. Boiling cinnamon bark in water will extract the flavor faster than steeping and make it much more concentrated. Boiling also releases other chemicals from the bark; this makes the extract taste bitter instead of sweet.

Ginger comes from the root of a reed-like plant belonging to the species *Zingiber officinale,* which is native to Southeast Asia. Ginger can be used fresh. It also can be dried and ground, or the flavor can be extracted by placing cut ginger in water. Steeping the root in hot water is not as effective as boiling. Boiling releases a sharp, pungent extract, which can be used to make ginger ale and ginger teas.

Our Findings

1. The longer the samples were boiled, the stronger the flavor and scent and the darker the color of the extract.
2. The longer the samples were steeped, the stronger the flavor and scent and the darker the color of the extract.
3. Boiling the cinnamon produced an extract with a stronger, bitter flavor. Steeping created a more delicate, sweeter flavor. Steeping the ginger released only a small amount of flavor, while boiling it created an extract that had a rich, pungent flavor.

HOW SWEET IT IS

While some people like their foods hot and spicy, others prefer to eat things that are sweet. Many fruits and vegetables are naturally sweet. Most plants contain at least some sugar; along with oxygen, sugar is the main product of photosynthesis. Over the years, people have learned how to remove and concentrate plant sugars. Sugar is a type of simple carbohydrate that comes in different forms. Most fruits get their sweetness from a sugar called fructose. Common table sugar is called sucrose, and it can be extracted from several plants. Sucrose is used as a sweetener in a range of food products, including soft drinks, candies, cakes, and cereals. One major source of sucrose is the sugar beet. In **Experiment 19:** *Extracting Sugar from Beets*, you will have the opportunity to make a sweet discovery as you extract some sugar from beets.

Sugar beets are plants whose roots contain a high concentration of sucrose. The European Union, the United States, and Russia are the three largest sugar beat producers in the world. Beet sugar accounts for 30% of the world's sugar production.

Extracting Sugar from Beets

Topic

How is natural sugar extracted from beets?

Introduction

Sucrose, or common table sugar, is one of the most important food products in the world. More than half of the processed sugar sold in the world today is extracted from a reed-like plant called sugar cane. This plant is native to tropical and subtropical climates. In India, people have been using it to crystallize sugar for more than 2,000 years. For hundreds of years, the only way that people in colder climates could enjoy sugar was to import it from the tropics. In the mid-1700s, however, German chemist Andreas Marggraf discovered that the sugar beet contained the same type of sugar as sugar cane. Within 50 years, commercial beet-sugar refineries began operating in Europe. In this activity, you will extract and concentrate sugar from the red beet, a relative of the sugar beet, using a process similar to that used in large-scale sugar refineries today.

Time Required

90 minutes

Materials

- 1-cup (500-mL) measuring cup or beaker
- watch or timer
- 2 or 3 small, fresh beets (not pickled or canned)
- sharp kitchen knife
- cutting board
- 2-qt saucepan with cover
- 1-qt saucepan
- large wooden spoon

- teaspoon

- strainer

- oven mitt

- 2 pot holders

- potato masher

- stove or hot plate

- adult to assist you

Safety Note This experiment should be conducted under the guidance of a responsible adult. During this experiment, you will be cooking on the stove and using a sharp knife to slice the beets. Be very careful not to spill the beet juice on clothes or carpets; it can leave permanent stains. Please review and follow the safety guidelines before proceeding.

Procedure

1. Before starting the experiment, cut the tops off the beets. Wash the beets thoroughly in the sink to remove any soil. Pour 2 cups (1 L) of water into the large saucepan and place it on the stove. Turn the heat on high and bring the water to a boil. Cut the beets into thin slices until you have about 1 cup (500 mL) of sliced beets. Observe the color and texture of the beets before you put them in the pot. Once the water in the saucepan starts boiling, add the beet slices and cover the pot. Turn the heat down to medium and allow the beets to simmer for 30 minutes.

2. After the beet slices have cooked, remove the pot from the stove and place it on a pot holder. Using an oven mitt, carefully remove the cover and use the potato masher to crush up the beets. Cover the pot and allow the mashed beets to sit in the hot water for 10 minutes. Slowly pour the water with the crushed beets through the strainer and into the second smaller saucepan (see Figure 1). Observe the color of the water and the color and texture of the beet mash as it collects in the strainer. After the beets have drained, dispose of the mash in the trash. Place the small saucepan back on the stove over medium heat and allow it to simmer uncovered for another 30 minutes.

3. As the beet juice cooks, stir it every few minutes with the wooden spoon to keep it from sticking to the bottom of the pot. After 30 minutes, turn off the stove and allow the pot to cool for 10 minutes. Carefully pour the

Oven mitt

Large saucepan

Mashed beets
and water mixture

Strainer

Small saucepan

Figure 1

© Infobase Publishing

beet juice from the pot back into the measuring cup. As you pour the juice, observe its consistency. Smell the juice in the measuring cup and taste it by dipping in a clean finger.

Analysis

1. How did the color and texture of the beets change after they were cooked?
2. How did the water change after the beets cooked in them for 30 minutes?
3. How did the beet juice change as it continued to cook on the stove after the beets were removed?
4. What did the beet juice look like, and how did it taste after you poured it back into the measuring cup at the end of Step 3?

What's Going On?

Sugar cane is still the number-one source of sucrose in the world, but sugar beets are closing in fast. Sugar beets are related to red beets. Rather than red, a sugar beet is a light tan color and looks more like a potato. Sugar beets also have a higher concentration of sugar in their cells, compared with red beets. After sugar beets are harvested from the fields, they are washed and their tops are removed. The tops are used as feed for cattle and other animals. After they are cleaned, the beets are sliced into thin strips called cossettes. The cossettes are placed in hot water and crushed. The water removes the sugar from the cells. The beet pulp is then drained and dried, and used for animal feed. The beet juice, with the sugar in it, is placed in a large tank and heated again. The water evaporates and concentrates the sugar. After a while, the beet juice turns into a thick, sweet syrup called molasses, which is what you made in this activity. The molasses is then processed further to purify and extract the sugar, which is crystallized and sold.

Our Findings

1. After the beets cooked, they became softer and paler.

2. The water that the beets cooked in turned red.

3. As the beet juice continued to cook on the stove, it became thicker and sticky.

4. The processed beet juice looked like dark red syrup that tasted sweet.

NATURAL AND ARTIFICIAL SWEETENERS

Sugar is great for sweetening foods and beverages, but it does have one major problem: It adds a great many "empty" calories to our diet. About ¼ teaspoon (1 gram) of sugar is 4 calories. This does not sound like much, but it adds up in a hurry. A typical 12-ounce (355-mL) can of soda has about 39 grams of sugar, which is equal to 140 calories or roughly 9 teaspoons of sugar! If you analyze the amount of sugar found in other snacks and foods, such as cereal and bread, you would be amazed at how much processed sugar you actually consume in a day. According to a 2009 study by the American Heart Association, the average American teenager eats about 34 teaspoons of refined sugar every day.

Previously, we discussed the dietary role of carbohydrates, including sugar. When sugars don't get used for energy, the body converts them into fat. This conversion can lead to weight gain. To help people keep the weight off, chemists have come up with a variety of artificial sweeteners that taste as sweet as (or sweeter than) sugar, but have far fewer calories. Even though they may produce a sweet taste, artificial sweeteners do not work the same way as sugar when they enter our bodies. In **Experiment 20:** *Testing Artificial Sweeteners*, you will compare two common artificial sweeteners with sugar to see how they affect a simple living organism.

EXPERIMENT 20 Testing Artificial Sweeteners

Topic

How does yeast behave in the presence of artificial sweeteners?

Introduction

All living things need energy to survive. Most plants get their energy from the Sun. Humans and other animals get energy from eating complex chemical compounds. Yeast is a simple, one-celled organism that gets energy from compounds that contain sugar. As yeast lives and grows, it releases carbon dioxide. This is why yeast is added to bread dough. Many bread recipes also call for the addition of molasses, corn syrup, or some other sugar-based compound to act as food for the yeast. As the yeast feeds on the sugary compounds in the dough, it produces bubbles of carbon dioxide gas. The bubbles get trapped in the dough, causing it to rise. This makes the bread fluffy.

Over the years, scientists have discovered a number of chemical compounds that are now used as artificial sweeteners. They make the food taste sweet without adding extra calories. In this activity, you will test to see the effects of two artificial sweeteners on the growth of yeast.

Time Required

60 minutes

Materials

- 3 clean, clear, plastic 1-liter soda bottles
- 3 identical 9-in. or 12-in. round latex balloons
- 3 packets of dry activated yeast (available in groceries in baking aisle)
- 3 large (12-oz) paper cups
- 3 plastic teaspoons
- measuring cup

- marker

- masking tape

- warm water

- timer or watch

- funnel

- 2 packets sugar

- 2 packets aspartame sweetener (Equal or similar brand)

- 2 packets sucralose sweetener (Splenda)

- glass of water for drinking

Safety Note Make certain that the teaspoons and paper cups are clean before tasting the sweetened water solutions. Do not drink the yeast mixtures. After the experiment, flush the yeast mixtures down the toilet. Please review and follow the safety guidelines before proceeding.

Procedure

1. Using the marker and tape, label one soda bottle and one cup "Sugar." Label another bottle and cup "Aspartame" and a third bottle and cup "Sucralose." Place the bottles and cups on the counter in front of you.

2. Fill each cup with 500 mL (8 oz) of warm (not hot) water and place a clean teaspoon in each cup. Empty two packets of sugar into the cup labeled "Sugar" and stir until the crystals dissolve. Repeat the procedure with the other two cups, making certain that you use the correct sweetener in each cup and a different spoon to stir each mixture.

3. Using the teaspoons, taste a small amount of each sweetened solution. Between tastes, take a sip of regular water to rinse your mouth. Compare the sweetness of the solutions and record your observations on the data table.

4. Use the funnel to empty one packet of dry yeast into each soda bottle. Rinse the funnel with clean water. Use the funnel to pour the water from the cup labeled "Sugar" into the bottle labeled "Sugar." Place one of the balloons on top of the bottle so that it looks like Figure 1. Gently shake the bottle back and forth to mix the yeast with the water. Do not get any of the mixture into the balloon. Rinse the funnel in clean water and dry it before repeating the procedure with the other two soda bottles. Allow all three bottles to stand undisturbed for 15 minutes. Observe the bottles. Wait another 15 minutes and observe the bottles again. Record your observations on the data table.

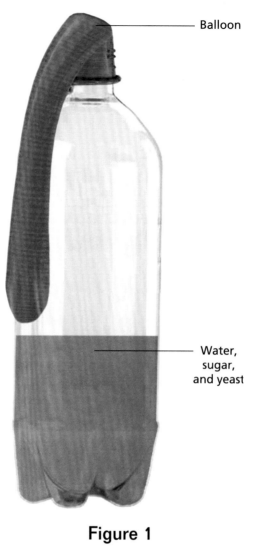

Balloon

Water,
sugar,
and yeast

Figure 1

© Infobase Publishing

Analysis

1. How did the sweetness of the three solutions compare with one another?

2. How did the mixtures in the three bottles look after 30 minutes?

3. Which solution made the balloon inflate the most? The least?

4. Based on your observations, what would be the results if you used either aspartame or sucralose in place of sugar or molasses while baking bread?

Data Table 1			
	Sugar Solution	Aspartame Solution	Sucralose Solution
Taste test			
Yeast 15 minutes			
Yeast 30 minutes			

What's Going On?

Aspartame and sucralose are chemical compounds used in place of sugar to sweeten beverages and snacks. Aspartame was discovered in 1965. It is about 200 times sweeter than sugar. Sucralose is made from sugar. It was discovered in 1976 and is 600 times sweeter than sugar. In this experiment, the yeast in the bottle with the sugar solution quickly began producing carbon dioxide gas and foamed up quite a bit. The yeast with the aspartame solution produced only a small amount of gas. The solution with the sucralose produced more gas than the aspartame solution but only about half as much as the sugar. This shows that even though sucralose is made from sugar, it does not have the same chemical composition and does not behave the same in living things.

Our Findings

1. Both the aspartame and the sucralose tasted much sweeter than the sugar.

2. The bottle with the sugar solution had the most bubbles and foamed up quite a bit. The bottle with the sucralose had a moderate amount of foam and the bottle with the aspartame only had a small amount of foam.

3. The balloon on the bottle with the sugar solution inflated the most. The one with the aspartame solution inflated only a little.

4. Adding sucralose to the dough in place of sugar would produce bread that tasted sweeter but was less airy than bread made with sugar. The bread made with aspartame would also be sweet, but it would be very dense because the dough would have not have risen much.

SALT OF THE EARTH

To a chef or a person who likes to eat French fries, salt is usually thought of as the little white crystals that you add to food to give it just the right flavor. To a chemist, however, salt has a very special meaning. Salts form when acids and bases react with each other. There are hundreds of different salts, but the most common is sodium chloride. It has the chemical formula $NaCl$. Sodium chloride is commonly called table salt. It has been used in food preparation for thousands of years. In **Experiment 21: Salt Reactions**, you will test to see the effect of salt on several foods.

EXPERIMENT 21   Salt Reactions

Topic

What effect does salt have on different foods?

Introduction

Common table salt, or sodium chloride, is the most abundant salt found on Earth. Not only is it the main salt found in seawater, but it also can be found in vast mineral deposits underground. Salt has two main roles in food preparation. First, it is used as a seasoning and is frequently added to sauces, stews, breads, and meat. Salt also is used in the preservation of food. Long before people had freezers and refrigerators, they used salt to cure meats and other foods that they wanted to store for extended periods of time. In this activity, you will discover why salt is such a good preservative when you test its effect on vegetables.

Time Required

45 minutes

Materials

- 2 large disposable plastic plates
- shaker of salt
- sharp kitchen knife
- cutting board
- marker
- fresh cucumber
- head of romaine lettuce
- large raw carrot
- roll of paper towels

- timer or watch

- adult to assist you

Safety Note This experiment should be done under the guidance of a responsible adult. You will be using a knife to cut slices out of raw vegetables. Please review and follow the safety guidelines before proceeding.

Procedure

1. Cut the cucumber and carrot into thin, round slices (i.e., cut through their middle). Each slice should be about ¼ in. (½ cm) thick. Pat each slice dry with a paper towel and divide the slices evenly between the two plates. Tear off four large lettuce leaves and place two leaves on each plate. Examine the vegetables on each plate and observe their texture and firmness. The set-up should look like Figure 1.

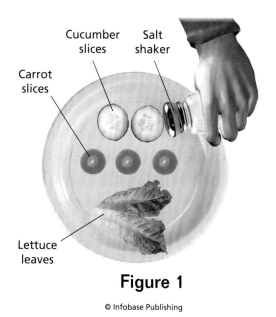

Cucumber slices   Salt shaker

Carrot slices

Lettuce leaves

Figure 1

© Infobase Publishing

2. Use the marker to label one plate "With Salt" and the other plate "Without Salt." Sprinkle salt on both sides of all the vegetables on the plate labeled "With Salt."

3. Place both plates in a safe location out of direct sunlight for 30 minutes. Then observe both sets of vegetables. Pay attention to their texture and firmness, and note whether there is any moisture present.

Analysis

1. What changes happened to the unsalted vegetables after 30 minutes?
2. What changes happened to the salted vegetables after 30 minutes?
3. How does salting affect the moisture content of foods?
4. How does salting help to preserve foods?

What's Going On?

Common table salt has some interesting chemical properties. One of the most important is that it is hygroscopic, meaning that it attracts and absorbs water. People discovered long ago that salt pulls water out of the air, or out of cut-up vegetables. Fruits and vegetables are mostly water. The salt caused some of this water to flow out of cells, forming little puddles on the plate. As the water left the cells, the plants became limp and soft.

It is not clear when people first discovered that salt could be used to preserve food, but they have been doing it for at least 5,000 years. Salting meat helps to speed the drying process. It also creates an environment that is hostile for most bacteria and other organisms that can spoil the food. It is interesting to note that food is not the only thing preserved by salting. When the ancient Egyptians wanted to preserve their dead, they packed the bodies in a substance called natron, which is mostly salt.

Our Findings

1. The unsalted vegetables changed very little after 30 minutes.
2. After 30 minutes, the salted vegetables became limp and soft, and the plates had wet spots.
3. Salting removes the moisture from foods.
4. Drying out the food makes it difficult for bacteria and other pathogens to live and spoil the food.

BEWARE OF SWEET AND SALTY

Both sugar and salt help to improve the flavor of foods, but too much of either one can lead to some serious health problems. Eating sugary foods adds extra calories. Any calories not used immediately are stored as fat. Obesity is on the rise in many countries, especially among children. Many scientists believe that a big part of the cause lies in the extra sugar that people eat. Over time, obese people are at greater risk for developing diabetes. People with diabetes cannot regulate the level of glucose in their blood. Left unchecked, diabetes can lead to blindness, loss of circulation, and even death.

Eating too much salt also can be hazardous to your health. The recommended daily allowance of salt is about $\frac{1}{5}$ oz (5 g) a day. This is about one teaspoon. In the United States, many people easily consume five times that amount every day. Not all the salt we eat comes from a salt shaker. Many processed foods—such as hot dogs, frozen pizza, and canned soup—contain a large amount of salt. Excess salt in the diet can cause a person's body to retain water. Over time, it can lead to high blood pressure, which is a risk factor for many other problems, such as heart attacks, kidney disease, and stroke.

One interesting fact about both salt and sugar is that our taste for extremely high levels of them seems to be acquired. People who traditionally eat diets low in processed sugar and salt don't miss the taste. When people regularly eat foods that are very sweet or salty, they want more of the same. That is a recipe for disaster. So put down the salt shaker, hide the sugar bowl, and read those nutritional labels!

Sauces, Soups, and Stews

Liquids play many important roles in the kitchen. We've already seen how cooking foods in boiling water can remove flavors and sugar, as well as how liquids such as vinegar can bring about a variety of chemical changes. In this chapter, we will concentrate on the importance of liquids as part of the meal.

SOLUTIONS, SOLVENTS, AND SOLUBILITY

Not only is water a nutrient, but it also plays a critical role in the preparation and cooking of food. If we didn't have water, it would be impossible to make soup, stew, or even a nice cup of tea. One reason that water is important in cooking is that it is an excellent **solvent.** A solvent is a substance (often a liquid) into which another substance is **dissolved.** The material being dissolved is called the **solute.** If you take a teaspoon of sugar and stir it into a glass of water, the sugar seems to disappear. If you taste the water, it will be sweet; the sugar is still there, but its molecules have blended with those of the water. The sugar water is now called a **solution.** In this case, the water is the solvent, the sugar is the solute, and the two combine to make a solution. In **Experiment 22: *Dissolving Salt and Sugar,*** you will test to see how the temperature of water affects its ability to dissolve sugar and salt crystals.

EXPERIMENT 22

Dissolving Salt and Sugar

Topic

How does the temperature of water affect its ability to dissolve salt and sugar?

Introduction

Water is often called "the universal solvent" because it can dissolve many substances, including sugar and salt. When salt or sugar crystals dissolve in water, they form a solution. If all the crystals disappear, the solution is said to be unsaturated. This means that the water in the solution could dissolve more salt or sugar in it. If you keep mixing salt or sugar into the water, you will eventually reach a point at which the solid can no longer dissolve. Instead of disappearing into the solution, the additional crystals begin to settle to the bottom of the container. When this happens, the solution is saturated. In this activity you will test to see if water's temperature has any effect on its ability to act as a solvent and if the solubility of salt and sugar are the same.

Time Required

1 hour prep before experiment, 45 minutes for the experiment

Materials

- 6 large (12-oz) clear drinking glasses or 1-L beakers
- measuring cup
- container of salt
- container of granulated sugar
- water
- teaspoon
- masking tape
- marker

- 2 clean, 2-L soda bottles with caps

- refrigerator or cooler with ice

- tea kettle or large saucepan

- hot plate or stove

- pot holder or oven mitt

- adult to assist you

Procedure

1. One hour before conducting the experiment, fill the two bottles with water and cap them. Place one bottle in a cooler full of ice or in a refrigerator and place the second bottle on a counter out of direct sunlight so that it reaches room temperature.

Salt-cold   Salt-warm   Salt-hot   Sugar-cold   Sugar-warm   Sugar-hot

Figure 1

2. Use the masking tape and marker to label the six glasses: "salt-cold," "salt-warm," "salt-hot," "sugar-cold," "sugar-warm," and "sugar-hot." Line up the six glasses on a counter or table as in Figure 1. Fill the tea kettle with water and place it on the stove or hot plate over medium heat. Allow it to heat until it is just below the boiling point.

3. Fill each glass marked "cold" with 1 cup (500 mL) of the refrigerated water. Fill each glass labeled "warm" with 1 cup of room-temperature water. Fill each glass labeled "hot" with 1 cup of water from the tea kettle.

4. Fill the teaspoon with salt. Make sure the salt is level across the top of the teaspoon. Place the salt into the "salt-cold" glass and stir until the salt crystals disappear. Add a second teaspoon of salt and stir again. Watch to see if all the salt goes into solution. Continue to add teaspoons of salt until you see salt crystals settling at the bottom of the glass. At this point, the solution is saturated. Record the number of teaspoons of salt that dissolved before the water became saturated on the data table. Then repeat the same procedure with the hot water and the warm water. After you have added salt to all three glasses, repeat the entire procedure with the sugar.

Data Table 1	
Cups	**Number of Teaspoons Dissolved**
Salt–hot water	
Salt–warm water	
Salt–cold water	
Sugar–hot water	
Sugar–warm water	
Sugar–cold water	

Analysis

1. Which temperature of water dissolved the most salt and sugar before becoming saturated?
2. Based on your results, what is the relationship between the temperature of water and its ability to dissolve solids?
3. Which solid was most affected by the change in temperature?
4. What would happen to the sugar in solution if you took the glass with hot water and placed it in the refrigerator?

 ## What's Going On?

As the temperature of water increases, it can dissolve more solids. As a result, more salt and sugar can go into solution in hot water than in cold. This is partly because hot water has more thermal energy. That energy helps to break the bonds that hold the crystals together. Even though both salt and sugar are more soluble in hot water, the difference in the solubility is not the same for each substance. While the ability of sugar to dissolve in water varies greatly with temperature, water temperature has only a small effect on salt. The difference in solubility has to do with the strength of the bonds holding the crystals together and the way the molecules are arranged. If a saturated solution of sugar and water is allowed to cool, solid particles come out of solution in a process called precipitation. If the cooling process is slow, and the water is allowed to evaporate, the sugar will form large crystals: rock candy.

Our Findings

1. The hot water was able to dissolve the most sugar and salt.
2. The higher the water temperature, the greater the ability of the water to dissolve solids.
3. The change in water temperature affected the ability of the sugar to dissolve more than the ability of the salt.
4. As the water cools, some of the sugar comes out of solution and settles to the bottom.

SOLUTIONS AND SUSPENSIONS

Not every liquid mixture is a solution. A true solution does not separate. The salt water and sugar water that you made in the previous experiment are both examples of solutions. In a solution, once the different components have mixed, they stay mixed unless the temperature changes or the water evaporates and a precipitate forms. Many of the liquid mixtures that we make in the kitchen are not solutions; they are **suspensions.** In **Experiment 23:** *Solutions and Suspensions*, you will make two liquid mixtures that will allow you to compare the properties of a suspension to that of a solution.

EXPERIMENT
23 Solutions and Suspensions

Topic

How can you tell a solution from a suspension?

Introduction

Solutions and suspensions are two types of homogeneous mixtures. A homogeneous mixture is one that has the same composition, no matter where you sample it. A cup of unsweetened tea is a good example of a homogeneous mixture. From the first sip to the last, it tastes the same; the concentration of tea is the same throughout the cup. A cup of tea also is an example of a solution. In a solution, all the components are in the same state and cannot be separated from one another mechanically (such as by using a filter). When the tea is first brewed, the hot water dissolves some substances from the leaves, which then mix with the water. If you were to pour the tea through a filter, the tea would go right through without separating.

A suspension is also a homogeneous mixture, but it is in two distinct states. An example of a suspension would be muddy water. Mud is made of tiny solid particles that are small enough to stay suspended in the water. Because a suspension is made up of two different states of matter, it can usually be separated by mechanical means. If you pour muddy water through a very fine filter, the water will pass through, but many of the solid particles will get trapped in the filter. In this activity, you will compare two common liquids to see some of the other differences between a solution and a suspension.

Time Required

45 minutes

Materials

- 2 large (12-oz) clear drinking glasses

- measuring cup

- container of skim or fat-free milk

- container of powdered chocolate drink mix
- container of Kool-Aid or similar powdered drink mix
- water
- 2 coffee filters
- small strainer
- small mixing bowl
- 2 teaspoons
- timer or watch
- flashlight

Safety Note Please review and follow the safety guidelines before proceeding.

Procedure

1. Use the measuring cup to pour 1 cup (500 mL) of water into one glass and 1 cup (500 mL) of fat-free milk into the other glass. Turn on the flashlight and place it against the glass with the water (see Figure 1). Observe the beam from the side as it goes through the glass. Repeat the procedure with the milk.

2. Place 1 teaspoon of chocolate powder into the glass with the milk. Sir vigorously for 30 seconds and allow the glass of chocolate milk to stand undisturbed for 10 minutes. Place one teaspoon of Kool-Aid drink mix into the glass filled with water and repeat the procedure.

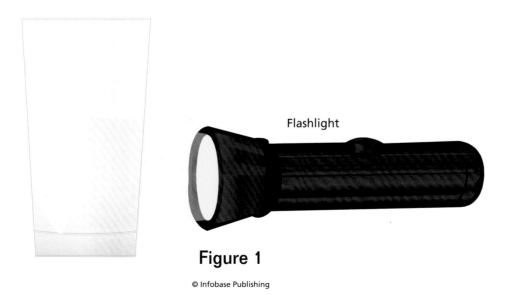

Flashlight

Figure 1

3. After 10 minutes have passed, turn on the flashlight and place it against the glass with the Kool-Aid. Observe the beam from the side as it goes through the glass. Repeat the procedure with the chocolate milk.

4. Place a coffee filter inside the strainer and place the strainer in the bowl (see Figure 2). Pour the Kool-Aid through the filter and allow it to filter for five minutes. Then remove the filter and pour off any remaining liquid. Look inside the filter after you have poured off the liquid. Repeat the procedure with the chocolate milk.

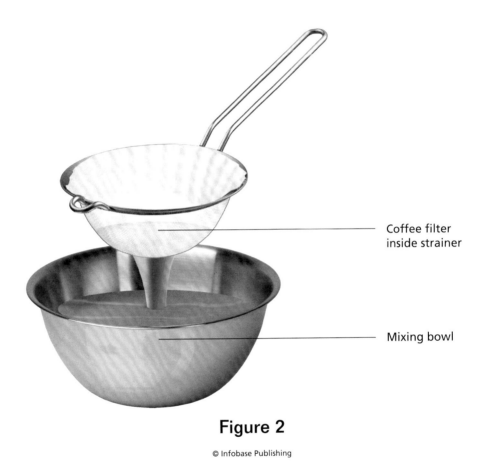

Coffee filter
inside strainer

Mixing bowl

Figure 2

© Infobase Publishing

Analysis

1. How did the flashlight beam appear when it went through the water and the plain milk? How did it change when you tried it with the Kool-Aid and the chocolate milk?

2. Which mixture filtered faster, the chocolate milk or the Kool-Aid?

3. After you poured off the liquid in Step 3, how did the filter look for both the chocolate milk and the Kool-Aid?

4. Which mixture was the suspension, and which was the solution?

What's Going On?

In this activity, the chocolate milk was a suspension and the Kool-Aid was a solution. When the flashlight was placed against the glass of Kool-Aid the light beam went right through without being blocked or scattered. When the Kool-Aid was filtered, it flowed quickly through the filter without separating at all. When you shined the light through the chocolate milk, the beam was blocked and scattered by the solid chocolate particles floating in the milk. When you poured the chocolate milk into the filter, the filter quickly became clogged by the chocolate particles. At the bottom of the glass, you could see a darker layer of milk where the chocolate had begun to settle.

Our Findings

1. The flashlight beam passed right through the water and the plain milk. It also passed through the Kool-Aid but was scattered by the chocolate milk.

2. The Kool-Aid passed through the filter much faster than the chocolate milk did.

3. The filter used for the chocolate milk had a brown color. The filter used for the Kool-Aid was clear.

4. The chocolate milk is a suspension, and the Kool-Aid is a solution.

MIXING LIQUIDS

Suspensions don't always involve mixing a solid and a liquid. You also can mix two liquids. Orange juice can be mixed with milk to make a tasty treat known as an Orange Julius. Two liquids will mix only if they have the same type of chemistry. Both orange juice and milk are water soluble, so they will naturally mix together. Mixing two liquids that have different chemical structures can lead to some interesting results. In **Experiment 24: *Mixing Oil and Vinegar*,** you will mix some classic Italian salad dressing and in the process see what happens when liquids with two different chemical compositions are mixed together.

Oil is not water soluble. The old saying "like mixing oil and water" refers to the idea of putting two opposites together.

EXPERIMENT 24 Mixing Oil and Vinegar

Topic

How can oil and vinegar be made to mix?

Introduction

Italian dressing tastes great on salads but can be a real problem to make. The two basic ingredients are oil and vinegar, with some spices mixed in for flavor. The problem happens when you try to mix the oil and vinegar. Oil is a non-polar compound, and vinegar is a polar compound. One general rule of chemistry is that polar compounds and non-polar compounds will not stay mixed unless there is another chemical to help them stay together. The third chemical is called an emulsifier. In this experiment, you will "whip up" some special salad dressing and in the process create a common emulsion that is found in most refrigerators.

Charged heads

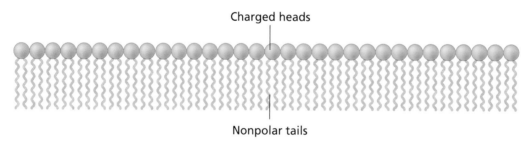

Nonpolar tails

Figure 1

© Infobase Publishing

Time Required

45 minutes

Materials

- cooking oil
- vinegar

- raw egg

- small deep mixing bowl

- wire whisk

- clear glass or plastic measuring cup

- timer or watch

- person to assist you

> **Safety Note** Handling raw eggs lead to the transfer of bacteria. After completing the experiment, wash your hands and all surfaces with hot soapy water. Discard the dressing when the experiment is finished. Do not eat it. Please review and follow the safety guidelines before proceeding.

Procedure

1. Use the measuring cup to pour about ¼ cup (125 mL) of vinegar and about ¼ cup (125 mL) of cooking oil into the bowl. Observe what happens to the oil and vinegar when they mix.

2. Use the whisk to vigorously beat the oil and vinegar mixture for one minute. Take turns with your assistant so you don't get tired. Observe the appearance of the mixture when you stop stirring.

3. Pour the mixture from the bowl back into the measuring cup and allow the mixture to stand undisturbed for three minutes. Observe what happens to the mixture as it stands.

4. Pour the mixture from the measuring cup back into the bowl. Crack the egg on the side of the bowl and add it to the oil and vinegar mixture. Repeat Steps 2 and 3 and note any changes that happen to the behavior of the mixture after you added the egg.

Analysis

1. What happened to the oil and vinegar when you first mixed them together?

2. How did the appearance of the mixture change after you beat the mixture the first time?

3. What happened to the plain oil and vinegar as it stood in the measuring cup?

4. What happened to the mixture of oil and vinegar and egg after you beat it?

5. What happened to the oil, vinegar, and egg mixture after it was allowed to stand for three minutes?

 ## What's Going On?

Anyone who has ever made Italian dressing knows that oil and vinegar do not stay mixed, no matter how hard you shake them. Eventually the oil droplets attract each other to form one large pool of oil. Because oil is less dense then vinegar, it floats to the top of the mixture. Oil and vinegar can be made to stay mixed if they are turned into an emulsion. An emulsion is a type of suspension. Tiny droplets of one substance (in this case, the oil) are dispersed and suspended in another substance (in this case, the vinegar). This is done with the help of an emulsifier. In this experiment, the egg yolk served as the emulsifier. Egg yolk is made of 50% water, 16% protein, and 33% fat. Most of the fat belongs to a class of chemicals called phospholipids. The molecules of phospholipids have an unusual shape. They have a polar "head" and a non-polar "tail" (see Figure 1). The non-polar tails align themselves around the non-polar oil droplets. The polar heads attract the vinegar, which is also polar, and the mixture stays mixed.

In case you were wondering, the combination of vinegar, oil, and egg does have a special name. It's called mayonnaise, which itself is an emulsion.

Our Findings

1. The two liquids separated.
2. The two liquids mixed together to make a yellowish liquid.
3. As the oil and vinegar stood in the measuring cup, the two liquids began to separate.
4. The mixture with the egg has the color of orange juice with a little foam on top.
5. After standing for three minutes, the mixture with the egg in it still did not separate.

VIVA VISCOSITY

Liquids have one unique property that can affect the way they behave in sauces, soups, and stews. It's called **viscosity.** Viscosity refers to the rate at which a liquid flows. A thick stew or chowder is very viscous and flows slowly. A clear soup or broth is not very viscous. In many cases a chef will change the viscosity of a liquid by adding a thickener. Cornstarch and flour often are added to gravy to increase viscosity. In **Experiment 25:** *Viscosity Meltdown*, you will discover that there is more than one way to change the viscosity of a liquid in the kitchen.

Flour is among many ingredients that can be added to gravy to make it more viscous—thicker and lumpier.

Viscosity Meltdown

Topic

How does temperature affect the viscosity of different liquids?

Introduction

Viscosity is a measure of the resistance of flow in a liquid. Liquids that are very viscous—such as molasses, honey, and catsup—are extremely thick and flow slowly. Water, on the other hand, is not viscous at all and flows quite easily. In this experiment, you will test to see what role, if any, the temperature of a liquid has on its viscosity.

Time Required

45 minutes

Materials

- 6 small (6-oz) disposable plastic cups
- 3 large bowls
- measuring cup
- bottle of Karo or similar brand light corn syrup
- teaspoon
- ice cubes
- hot water
- timer or watch

Safety Note Please review and follow the safety guidelines before proceeding.

Procedure

1. Label six cups as follows: "cold water," "cold syrup," "room-temperature water," "room-temperature syrup," "warm water," and "warm syrup."

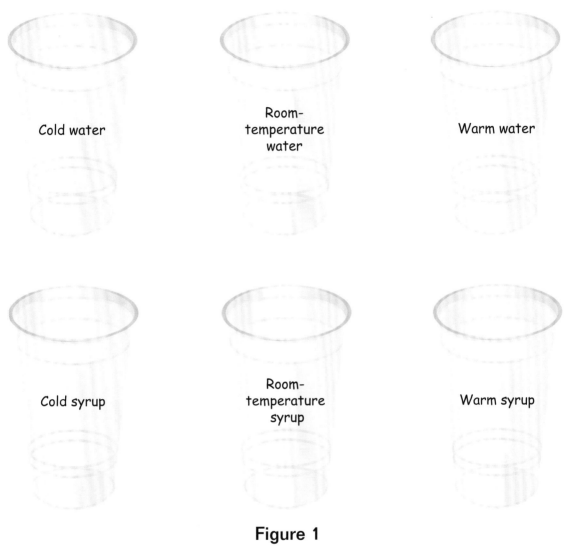

Cold water

Room-temperature water

Warm water

Cold syrup

Room-temperature syrup

Warm syrup

Figure 1

© Infobase Publishing

2. Use the measuring cup to pour ¼ cup (125 mL) of water into three of the plastic cups that are labeled as having water. Pour ¼ cup (125 mL) of corn syrup into the other three cups.

3. Place the "cold"-labeled cups of water and corn syrup in one of the large bowls. Pack ice cubes around the cups and fill the bowl with cold water, but don't allow the water to flow into the cups. Place the "warm"-labeled cups of water and corn syrup in the second large bowl and fill the bowl with hot (not boiling) water. Do not allow the water to flow into the cups. Leave the other cup of water and corn syrup on the table. Allow all of the cups to stand undisturbed for 10 minutes.

3. While pouring from the two "room temperature" cups that have been sitting on the table, time how many seconds it takes to pour both the corn syrup and then the water into the empty bowl. Record the times on the data table. Repeat the procedure with the two cups that were sitting in the ice bath and the two cups that were sitting in the hot water.

Data Table 1	
Solution Name	**Number of Seconds to Pour**
Cold water	
Room-temperature water	
Warm water	
Cold syrup	
Room-temperature syrup	
Warm syrup	

Analysis

1. What effect did temperature have on the time it took to pour the water?
2. What effect did temperature have on the time it took to pour the syrup?
3. How did the viscosity of the cold syrup compare to the viscosity of the warm syrup?
4. What problem would you encounter if you kept honey or molasses in the refrigerator?

What's Going On?

Viscosity can be thought of as the internal friction that occurs in a liquid when it flows. Some liquids, such as corn syrup or gravy, have a high viscosity; others, such as milk or soda, are not very viscous. Changes in temperature affect viscosity in different ways. As you discovered in this experiment, changing the temperature of water has almost no effect on its viscosity. It flows at the same speed, regardless of whether it is hot or cold. On the other hand, the viscosity of corn syrup is related to temperature. When corn syrup is cold, its viscosity is high, and it barely flows. Warm syrup flows more easily. This is why it's a good idea not to keep pancake syrup in the refrigerator. Otherwise, you might be late for school waiting for your syrup to flow out of the bottle. In many restaurants, pancake syrup is heated before it is served, making it easier for patrons to pour and enjoy.

Our Findings

1. Temperature had no effect on the pour rates of the water.
2. The cold syrup took much longer to pour than the warm syrup.
3. The cold syrup had a much higher viscosity than the warm syrup.
4. Keeping honey or molasses in the refrigerator would make it very difficult to pour because the viscosity would be too great.

GIVE ME THE GRAVY

Before we end this chapter on liquids in the kitchen, we need to take a look at the science behind one very special type of liquid: gravy. If you take a look at any good cookbook, you'll probably find several recipes for gravy. Some are white; some are brown; some use the drippings form meat; and others are based solely on vegetables. The one thing that almost every type of gravy has in common, however, is that it tends to be thick. Most gravies fall into a special category of mixture called a colloidal dispersion. They get their thickness from tiny, solid particles called **colloids**. A colloidal-sized particle is still too big to form a true solution, but it is small enough to pass through a normal filter. The word *colloid* is based on the Greek term *kolla,* which means "glue." Anyone who has ever eaten overly thick gravy knows that it does stick just like glue.

Two of the most common substances used to thicken gravy are flour and cornstarch. In order to make gravy appetizing, the thickening agent must be stirred evenly into a liquid that includes a certain amount of fat or oil. The fat coats the colloids and helps keep the gravy from being lumpy and dry. Also, it is important that only a small amount of thickener be used, usually only a tablespoon or two. Otherwise, instead of making gravy, you might wind up gluing your pasta together!

What the Future Holds

New advances in science and technology are always changing the way we live. This is particularly true when it comes to the production and processing of food. Over the past 20 years, biologists and chemists have gained a much deeper understanding of the inner workings of both living cells and the behavior of molecules. This information has given farmers, ranchers, and fishermen a range of new tools and techniques to help produce more food. Some of these technological advances have been helpful, but others have created new problems that are only now starting to surface. Here are a few of the questions that we will be facing when it comes to food production in the future.

GROWING GREEN: THE MOVE BACK TO ORGANIC FOOD PRODUCTION

In recent years, many farmers have decided to "go green" when it comes to the way they grow their crops and raise their livestock. However, this new movement is not the first green revolution that the world has experienced. The original green revolution took place more than 60 years ago, and in the eyes of many scientists it was anything but green.

These days, when people talk about "going green," they are usually referring to the act of following practices that reduce the environmental impact on the planet. "Green living" includes using energy-saving devices in our homes, driving a hybrid car instead of a gas guzzler, and buying organic foods. From a scientific standpoint, the term *organic* means anything that is or was living and contains the element carbon. In food production, however, *organic* generally refers to something that has been grown and/or produced without the use of pesticides, chemical fertilizers, or artificial additives. For thousands of years, organic agriculture was the only way that farmers could produce crops. Then, thanks to advances in science, the first "green revolution" took place in the 1940s, and things quickly changed.

The changes in agriculture during this time resulted primarily from work carried out in Mexico by Dr. Norman Borlaug. Dr. Borlaug was an American biologist who worked on breeding crops that produced higher yields and were more tolerant of disease and drought. When he began his research, Mexico had to import more than half of its wheat. Within 20 years, Mexico was producing so much wheat that it was exporting the grain to other countries. The results were so dramatic that in 1968, the director of the U.S. Agency for International Development stated that a "green revolution" had occurred. Following

Nobel Prize-winning biologist Dr. Norman Borlaug (shown in 1970) holds stalks of his specifically cross-bred wheat, which is designed to be more disease resistant to produce larger yields of wheat.

his success in Mexico, Dr. Borlaug and others began using the same techniques in Pakistan and India with similar results.

Better plants were only one reason for the green revolution. In order to produce such an enormous increase in food production, farmers had to change the way that they raised crops. They moved away from traditional organic farming techniques and began using chemical pesticides, inorganic fertilizers, and irrigation to make their plants grow. While these new technologies produced very impressive short-term results, they have led to some rather serious long-term problems. Let's first take a look at the effect of pesticides.

Pesticides are chemicals designed to kill insects, fungus, and bacteria that kill or damage plants. Since the earliest days of agriculture, farmers have been looking for ways to cut their crop losses. In 2500 B.C., Sumerian farmers were using sulfur compounds in their fields to help reduce the numbers of insects and mice that were eating their crops. Over the centuries, farmers have tried many different substances as pesticides with mixed results. In wasn't until the late 1800s, however, that chemists were able to begin creating more potent compounds to control pests, including DDT and arsenic-based compounds.

Many of these pesticides were good at killing pests, but they also killed other living things. Helpful insects, such as bees and wasps, were getting wiped out, as were larger animals that normally ate the pests. It was also discovered that many of the pesticides had a long life cycle and were being passed up the food chain to humans. DDT was eventually banned, but other potentially toxic compounds are still in use. Today, one of the biggest questions is what the long-term effects of some of these pesticides will be. Yet without these chemicals to control pests, it would be very difficult for modern farmers to keep producing crops at increased yields.

A second problem has been brought about by the widespread use of inorganic fertilizers. In **Experiment 1:** *How Soil Nutrients Affect Plant Growth*, we saw that plants grow best when they have the proper supply of nutrients from the soil. The idea that plants needed certain essential elements to grow was first published in 1731 by English farmer Jethro Tull (yes, that was a real person, not just the name of a rock band!) In 1840, German chemist Justus von Liebig came up with his Law of the Minimum, which stated that a plant's growth would be limited by the essential element that was present in the lowest or minimum amounts relative to its needs. He reasoned that if all the essential growth elements were increased by the right

British agriculturalist Jethro Tull was a pioneer who helped develop the British Agricultural Revolution. However, Tull's theories were not always correct. He mistakenly thought that pulverizing plants would activate nutrients in the soil and, thus, fertilizer was unnecessary. He later began using horse manure as fertilizer, after noting that it contained weed seeds.

amounts, plants would have unlimited growth potential.

Liebig was correct, but chemists were still trying to figure out what the essential elements were. Over the years, farmers had discovered that animal manure and compost acted as natural fertilizers. They helped to make plants grow, but scientists were not sure which chemical compounds were responsible. Over the next few decades, as technology progressed, scientists discovered which elements were needed by plants and began creating inorganic fertilizers with combinations of these essential elements.

Inorganic fertilizers contain the same chemicals as organic fertilizers. The big difference is the source of the chemicals and their concentrations. Most inorganic fertilizers come from either mineral salts or petroleum. They contain essential elements at much higher concentrations than what is in organic fertilizers. As a result, when inorganic fertilizers are applied to the soil, the plants can grow faster and be more productive.

The widespread use of inorganic fertilizers has led to several major problems, however. First, when fertilizers are applied, they don't stay on farmers' fields. When it rains or when fields are irrigated, fertilizers can run off into streams, rivers, and ponds, where they cause algae and weeds to grow rapidly. This growth can disrupt natural ecosystems and eventually create "dead zones," such as the one in the Gulf of Mexico near the mouth of the Mississippi River.

Even when they stay in the soil, inorganic fertilizers change the soil chemistry until plants cannot grow without a new supply of fertilizer each year. This forces farmers to continue fertilizing fields. Over time, mineral salts can begin to precipitate into the soil, causing the soil to lose its natural productivity. In some places, farmers have been using inorganic fertilizers for so many years that they have had to abandon their fields. Finally, many fertilizers are made from oil, and farmers need to use heavy machinery to apply them. This means that their use involves a great deal of energy consumption, as well as the release of carbon dioxide and other greenhouse gases.

In an attempt to reduce the negative environmental impact of pesticides and inorganic fertilizers, many farmers have returned to a more traditional method of growing crops. Instead of using chemical pesticides, organic farmers control insects and other pests with natural predators or other biological means. This generally means using other plants or animals to block or eat the organisms that are causing problems. Instead of inorganic fertilizers, organic farmers use compost and manure to help enrich their soil with nutrients. Another important step is to rotate crops so that the same plants aren't grown on the same soil year after year. Rotating helps to restore the natural chemical balance to the soil without having to use fertilizers.

Of course, there are drawbacks to organic farming. Crop yields for foods grown organically are usually much lower than for foods grown using inorganic growing techniques. In addition, organic farmers need to use more land to produce their food, and land is expensive. As a result, food grown organically usually costs more than food produced using inorganic methods. As with most issues, there is no easy answer. But all over the world, scientists are working in labs and fields to find new ways to meet the growing demand for food while preserving the natural environment.

AQUACULTURE: FARMING THE SEAS

Historians note that humans first started planting crops around 12,000 years ago. Before that time, most of the food that people ate was either hunted or gathered from wild sources. Today, many people still hunt, but they usually do it for sport rather than out of a need for food. The one major exception can be found in the ocean. When fishermen go out to sea, they are hunting for food. Hunting can be a hit-or-miss proposition. First, you have to find the intended target. Then you have to be talented or clever enough to catch it. Fishermen may spend a great deal of time and effort in search of a big catch, only to come up empty. This is especially true as the number of fish in natural populations continues to drop. These days, simply finding enough fish to catch can be a big problem.

In order to meet the growing demand for fresh seafood, some fishermen are putting away their nets and becoming farmers of the sea. The process is called **aquaculture,** and it uses some of the same techniques that ranchers and farmers use to raise animals on land. Aquaculture includes the breeding, rearing, and harvesting of plants and animals in many aquatic environments, including ponds, rivers, lakes, and the ocean. Nearly half the fish eaten by people around the world today are raised on farms.

Even though it is the fastest growing form of food production in the world today, aquaculture is not a new idea. People have been raising seafood for thousands of years. What is new is the scale of production and the science and technology being used. Modern aquaculture can be divided into several groups, depending on the type of organism being raised. Freshwater fish farming is the most common. Some of the varieties of fish raised by freshwater aquaculture include trout, catfish, carp, and tilapia. If you eat a fish sandwich at some larger fast-food chains, it is likely that you are eating fish raised on giant freshwater farms

Freshwater fish farms often are designed to be artificial environments. The fish are reared in large, concrete-lined ponds. Food and water quality are carefully monitored. When it comes time to harvest the fish, the ponds are drained, and bucket loaders scoop up the fish.

For saltwater species, things are a bit more complicated. Anyone who has ever tried to set up a salt-water aquarium knows that it is much more difficult to make an artificial ocean because you need to get the water chemistry just right. As a result, many marine aquaculture systems are designed to work in the natural ocean environment. Marine aquaculture, or "mariculture," includes the production of shellfish such as oysters, clams, mussels, and shrimp. It also includes certain fish, such as salmon. Most often, the sites selected for marine aquaculture are bays and harbors: places sheltered from waves and storms. Many mariculture systems use cages or pens. This not only keeps the fish in, but also keeps out some natural species and predators.

Overfishing has reduced some fish populations to dangerously low levels. In the past few decades, aquaculture has helped to take some of the pressure off these fish populations. Still, aquaculture is not without problems. In order for aquaculture to be profitable, the number of animals that must be confined in ponds or pens is often many times their natural population density. This has led to several serious problems. First, the animals themselves get stressed. (Just think of how you feel when you are forced to squeeze into a small area with a bunch of other people.) In many cases, animals will stop breeding, or begin fighting and cannibalizing one another. In addition, diseases spread quickly through the entire population. As a result, many aquaculture systems use preventive antibiotics, which can get passed up the food chain to the people who eat the fish. Recent studies have shown that the overuse of antibiotics has weakened the human ability to fight bacterial infections. It also has led to the development of so-called "super germs," which don't die when treated with regular antibiotics.

One final problem with having so many animals jammed together in a small space has to do with the waste they create. When you have thousands of fish "pooping" in the same place, the water quickly becomes polluted. This is not a big problem for freshwater fish farms because they filter the artificial ponds. In the natural marine environment, it is a real issue. It pollutes the water in the fish pens, as well as in the surrounding water. This can spread diseases to natural fish populations in the area.

Clearly, as the world's human population continues to grow and natural fish populations shrink, it will be up to aquaculture to help close the gap. The problem is to design aquaculture systems that have minimal impacts on the environment and the animals being raised. One solution is the use of integrated multi-trophic aquaculture, or IMTA for short. An IMTA system mimics a natural ecosystem. Several species are raised together. Ideally, the waste created by one species can then be used as the nutrients for another species. Because several species are living together, no one population is overcrowded. The main problem is that not every species fits nicely into an IMTA, but it is a start. As new scientific research into the behavior of fish and the dynamics of natural marine ecosystems becomes available, other new technologies will almost certainly be developed to move aquaculture forward.

THE GREAT SWEETENER DEBATE

We have discussed how eating too much sugar can lead to obesity, as well as other health conditions, such as diabetes. People love to eat sweets, though. One way that people have been able to enjoy sweet food without counting calories is through the use of artificial sweeteners, such as aspartame and sucralose. For a while it seemed as if science had come to the rescue of people with a sweet tooth, but unfortunately, not everyone is happy with the solution. Although using artificial sweeteners in place of sugar may help people control their weight, some researchers and consumer groups believe that these chemical copycats may also open the door for other health problems. This belief has led to controversy about the safety of artificial sweeteners.

In the United States, before any new additive can be used in food, it must first meet certain standards or guidelines. This is spelled out in a law known as the Federal Food, Drug, and Cosmetics Act. Any additive used in food must first be reviewed and approved by the U.S. Food and Drug Administration (FDA). If a substance has been used before in foods and has not appeared to cause health problems, then it is classified as GRAS, which means "Generally Recognized As Safe." If a substance is found to cause cancer in humans or other test animals, then it is not considered to be safe. In theory, it cannot be used as an additive in foods.

As part of the approval process, the FDA asks the company to submit reports showing that the substance is either made from compounds that are GRAS, or that extensive testing has been done on the substance. If the substance has no known safety record, the FDA usually requires that animal studies be conducted first. Scientists working in labs feed large doses of the substance to mice, rats, and other test animals and then wait to see how they react. If the animal studies prove safe, the FDA looks at other potential long-term effects on humans, including any harmful byproducts of the substance. Once all of the data have been reviewed, the FDA makes its decision. Either the substance is approved, or more tests are run.

Even if all the animal tests and reports show no problems, there is no guarantee that a substance will be 100% safe. Because of this, the FDA continues to monitor food additives and review any new scientific studies that may be run, even after approval. The FDA also operates the Adverse Reaction Monitoring System (ARMS) to serve as a safeguard for all food additives. The ARMS system allows the FDA to investigate complaints or reports of health issues related to additives in foods. If an additive is shown to cause health problems after it has been approved, the FDA can go back and ban it at a later date. This has already happened with one artificial sweetener known as cyclamate.

Cyclamate was discovered in the 1930s. It is about 50 times sweeter than sugar. It was originally approved, but several studies later reported that it caused cancer in test animals. Cyclamate was banned in the Untied States in 1970, but it was still approved for use in more than 50 other countries. Later tests on cyclamate failed to confirm that it caused cancer, and the manufacturer is trying to get the U.S. ban lifted.

Another artificial sweetener that has caused concern is saccharin. Saccharin was discovered in 1879. It was the first artificial sweetener to be used in foods. Later testing showed a link between saccharin and certain forms of cancer. In 1977, the FDA attempted to ban saccharin, as it had done with cyclamate. Because it was the only available artificial sweetener at the time, the attempt to ban caused a problem. Banning it would have meant the end of most "diet" foods. After much debate, the United States Congress overruled the FDA decision. Instead of banning saccharin, they insisted that all foods that contained the substance carry a warning label stating that saccharin was shown to cause cancer in laboratory animals. Over the next 20 years, tests on people who used saccharin seemed to show that they had no greater risk of getting cancer than anyone else. The warning label has now been dropped. In Canada, saccharin has been banned for general use, but diabetics can use it.

In recent years, the FDA has approved a number of new artificial sweeteners including aspartame and sucralose. Neither has a warning label, but many people (including some scientists) have raised concerns about long-term safety. People have sent complaints to ARMS about both sweeteners. Aspartame has been said to cause dizziness, headaches, and memory loss. Some researchers fear that it might increase the risk of multiple sclerosis and Alzheimer's disease. Sucralose does not appear to have as many problems as aspartame, but it is a newer product.

In the meantime, the search for better and safer artificial sweeteners has not stopped. Because the diet food industry is such a big business, any new discovery could be worth billions of dollars. New sweeteners, such as Neotame and Stevia, already have been developed. More are in the works. No one knows what the future will bring for these and other food additives, but as of right now, it does looks pretty sweet!

Glossary

acid   a chemical that reacts with a base to form a salt

amino acid   a chemical substance that acts as a building block for proteins, enzymes, and hormones

aquaculture   the breeding, rearing, and harvesting of plants and animals in an aquatic environment

base   a chemical that feels slippery in liquid form; a base reacts with an acid to form a salt.

Calorie   the amount of heat energy needed to raise the temperature of one gram of water by one degree Celsius

carbohydrates   nutrients composed of sugars, starch, and fiber; carbohydrates are the main source of energy for the body

chemical change   a permanent change in matter

cholesterol   a waxy, fatlike substance found in every cell membrane in the human body; cholesterol also is found in many of foods.

colloids   particles that are small enough to fit through a filter but do not dissolve in a solvent

conduction   the process of transferring heat in solid objects, such as from a stove burner to a pan; conduction happens relatively quickly.

consumer   an animal that gets its energy by eating another living thing

convection   the process of transferring heat in liquids and gases; convection is slower but more even than conduction.

dissolve   the process in which a solid combines with a liquid to form a solution

energy   the ability to do work or, make things move, grow, or change

fats   Nutrients made from fatty acids and glycerol; fats contain the most calories per gram (9).

fiber   carbohydrates that are not digested; fiber helps to regulate the movement of waste through the digestive system.

food chain   shows the process by which energy is passed from one living thing to another

food web   has the same purpose as a food chain, but allows for more complex relationships among many different organisms

heat   a form of thermal energy

Kilocalorie   one thousand calories; when used to measure the amount of stored energy in food, it is usually written as Calorie (with a capital "C").

lipid   fat

matter   any substance that has mass and takes up space

microbiology   the branch of science involved with the study of microscopic living things

minerals   inorganic substances found in food that the body uses as nutrients

nutrients   chemical substances necessary for life

nutrition   the science of determining which foods and substances are needed for healthy living

photosynthesis   the process used by green plants to manufacture food from sunlight, carbon dioxide, and water

physical change   a change in matter that usually can be reversed

producer   a living thing that uses photosynthesis to make food energy directly from the Sun

protein   nutrient that helps to build and maintain cell growth

radiation   the process of transferring heat using waves or pulses of energy, such as with a microwave oven

solute   in a solution, the substance dissolved by the solvent

solution   a mixture of solvent and solute

solvent   a liquid into which a substance can dissolve

starch   a complex carbohydrate found in food; it acts as the body's main source of energy.

sublimation   process that occurs when matter turns from a solid directly to a gas

sugar   a simple carbohydrate found in grains, milk, and fruit

suspension   a mixture in which the solid particles stay mixed, but never dissolve

temperature   measure of the amount of thermal energy contained in a substance

viscosity   a liquid's resistance to flow

vitamins   nutrients found in food; they contain compounds necessary for growth and good health.

yeast   single-celled fungi that release carbon dioxide gas when they feed on sugars

Bibliography

Brown, Alton. *I'm Just Here for the Food.* New York: Stewart, Tabori & Chang, 2002.

Dittman, Richard and Glenn Schmeig. *Physics In Everyday Life.* New York: McGraw Hill, 1979.

Editors of Consumers Guide. *How Things Work.* Lincolnwood, Ill.: Publications International Ltd., 1994.

Hewitt, Paul. *Conceptual Physics, 8th Edition.* New York: Addison Wesley, 1998.

Hill, John. *Chemistry for Changing Times, 4th Edition.* Minneapolis: Burgess Publishing Co., 1984.

Macaulay, David. *The Way Things Work.* Boston: Houghton Mifflin, 1988.

Mandell, Muriel. *Simple Kitchen Experiments.* New York: Sterling Publishing Co., 1993.

Suchocki, John. *Conceptual Chemistry.* New York: Addison Wesley, 2001.

Tomecek, Stephen. *Teaching Science Yes, You Can!* New York: Scholastic Teaching Resources, 2007.

——. *What A Great Idea! Inventions That Changed The World.* New York: Scholastic, 2002.

Further Resources

Brown, Alton. *Good Eats: The Early Years.* New York: Stewart, Tabori & Chang, 2009.

Brown, Alton. *I'm Just Here for the Food.* New York: Stewart, Tabori & Chang, 2002.

Cobb, Vicki. *See For Yourself: More Than 100 Experiments for Science Fairs and Projects.* New York: Scholastic, 2001.

D'Amico, Joan and Karen Drummond. *The Healthy Body Cookbook.* New York: John Wiley & Sons, 1999.

Parsons, Russ. *How to Read a French Fry and Other Stories of Intriguing Kitchen Science.* Boston: Houghton Mifflin, 2001.

Tomecek, Stephen. *Teaching Science Yes, You Can!* New York: Scholastic Teaching Resources, 2007.

Tomecek, Stephen. *What a Great Idea! Inventions That Changed the World.* New York: Scholastic, 2002.

VanCleave, Janice. *Food and Nutrition for Every Kid,* San Francisco: Jossey-Bass, 1999.

Wolke, Robert. *What Einstein Told His Cook: Kitchen Science Explained.* New York: W.W. Norton, 2002.

———. *What Einstein Told His Cook 2: The Sequel—Further Adventures in Kitchen Science.* New York: W.W. Norton, 2005.

Web Sites

The Accidental Scientist: Science of Cooking
http://www.exploratorium.edu/cooking/index.html
This Web site, hosted by the Exploratorium Science Center, invites visitors to explore some of the science behind various forms of cooking. It features webcasts, recipes, and many different experiments and activities that you can try.

Food Info
http://www.food-info.net/uk/index.htm
This is a great site if you are looking for information about different types of foods and cooking techniques. It features in-depth descriptions about food components, the production

of food, and food safety, as well as an extensive section on food allergies.

Everyday Mysteries: Fun Science Facts from the Library of Congress

http://www.loc.gov/rr/scitech/mysteries

This site, hosted by the Library of Congress, features the answers to hundreds of questions dealing with day-to-day phenomena, including questions on cooking and food. All questions were asked by researchers and answered by librarians from the Library's Science Reference Services.

How Artificial Sweeteners Work

http://recipes.howstuffworks.com/artificial-sweetener.htm

This site discusses the history and controversy surrounding artificial sweeteners. It includes a breakdown of different sweeteners, the dates of their discoveries, and the effects on our bodies.

NOAA Aquaculture Program

http://aquaculture.noaa.gov/

This site, presented by the National Oceanic and Atmospheric Administration, provides a good overview of the different types of aquaculture systems at work in the world today. It includes links to the latest research and technologies.

Picture Credits

Index

Page numbers in *italics* indicate photos or illustrations, and page numbers followed by *t* indicate tables.

About the Author

STEPHEN M. TOMECEK is a scientist who loves to eat and cook. When he is not experimenting in the kitchen, he is a nonfiction author who has written more than 40 books for both children and teachers, including *Bouncing & Bending Light,* the 1996 winner of the American Institute of Physics Science Writing Award. Tomecek also works as a consultant and writer for The National Geographic Society and Scholastic Inc.